Learning God's Stories Together

Learning God's Stories Together

Intergenerational Bible Study & Activities for Church & Home

Dorothy Henderson

with Lisa-Dawn McKenzie

The Presbyterian Church in Canada

Editor: Tim Faller
Cover and interior design: Margaret Kyle and Verena Velten
Proofreader: Merlin Beltain
Cover and interior artwork by Margaret Kyle, from *The Family Story Bible*.
Copyright © 1996 Wood Lake Publishing Inc.

Special thanks to Susan Samuel, Kincardine, Ontario; Mary Jane Bisset,
Goderich, Ontario; and Megan Purdy, Owen Sound, Ontario, who were
instrumental in dreaming this resource.

WoodLake is an imprint of Wood Lake Publishing, Inc. Wood Lake Publishing acknowledges the financial support of the Government of Canada,
through the Book Publishing Industry Development Program (BPIDP)
for its publishing activities. Wood Lake Publishing also acknowledges the
financial support of the Province of British Columbia through the Book
Publishing Tax Credit.

BRONZE

BNC CERTIFIED | BIBLIOGRAPHIC DATA 2007-08

At Wood Lake Publishing, we practise what we publish, being guided
by a concern for fairness, justice, and equal opportunity in all of our
relationships with employees and customers. Wood Lake Publishing is
an employee-owned company, committed to caring for the environment
and all creation. Wood Lake Publishing recycles, reuses, and encourages
readers to do the same. Resources are printed on 100% post-consumer
recycled paper and more environmentally friendly groundwood papers
(newsprint), whenever possible. A percentage of all profit is donated to
charitable organizations.

Library and Archives Canada Cataloguing in Publication

A catalogue record for this publication is available
from the National Library of Canada.

ISBN 978-1-5514-559-4

Published by WoodLake
An imprint of Wood Lake Publishing Inc.
9590 Jim Bailey Road, Kelowna, BC, Canada, V4V 1R2
www.woodlakebooks.com
250.766.2778

Printing 10 9 8 7 6 5 4 3 2 1
Printed in Canada by Houghton Boston

Table of Contents

Part 2: Four units of lessons for all-ages groups

Introduction

This book is about all ages learning together. It is about being receptive and open to learning with others, regardless of age.

Learning together in an all-ages group is one of the most rewarding things you will do in your congregation. It is fun and builds community. It challenges people in intergenerational groups to explore the Bible story and decide together how they can live out the story in day-to-day life.

Grace is a retired nurse who has never married or had children. But she enjoys children. She especially enjoys six-year-old Rachel, who sits beside her in church. Like all the other young children in worship, Rachel colours a picture that relates to the day's scripture reading. Grace watches her colouring with interest and curiosity.

Robert has a demanding career. He is downtown from 7 a.m. to 7 p.m. Still, when Sunday rolls around, Robert tries very hard to get out of bed and, together with his wife, take their two children to church. Robert went to church as a child, and he believes that a solid religious foundation is good to have. But Robert worries. Is he a good enough dad? Is he a good enough Christian? Should he spend more time with his children?

Sue and Jim are proud grandparents. The problem is, their only daughter and their only grandson live on the other side of the country. They must be content with a yearly visit, frequent e-mails, and phone calls. Sue and Jim miss children in their lives.

Although it is unusual in North America now, the Blandfords have five children. Not only is Dora Blandford a busy mother, but she also provides home schooling for the four oldest children. Now that Dora's oldest son is a teenager, he helps with tutoring the younger children in their studies.

Grace, Robert, Sue, Jim, and Dora are all adults who want to be with children as they grow and learn the Christian faith. Rachel, Robert's children, Sue and Jim's grandson, and Dora's five children also have something in common – they love being with adults. They like to learn with, from, and about adults. In fact, it is only adults who can help children and teens learn how to become adults.

Learning God's Stories Together is for adults who want to do Bible study and activities with children; it is for children who love to do things with adults; and it is for teens who want to be part of the group, even though they might not admit it! This book is about people – people who want to contribute to each other's growth in faith.

A unique community develops when Christians share common convictions and practices. It is rejuvenating and hopeful when all ages learn together. As Christians, we call this community a "covenant community." Deuteronomy 6:4–9 reminds us to recite and talk about God with our children and leave signs about God on our modern-day doorposts – fridges and bulletin boards.

This book has two parts. Part 1 explains the theory and practice of all-ages learning. Why do we want all-ages learning in our congregation or home? Who will participate? How and where and when will we organize intentional all-ages learning? Part 2 has 20 all-ages learning experiences. Each session offers suggestions for how people from several generations might explore together a biblical story, then live and work as Christians in the world because of that story.

PART 1

All-ages learning
and how it works

What is all-ages learning?

Several terms can be used for all-ages learning – intergenerational, cross-generational, multigenerational, holistic, or community-of-faith learning. Regardless of the term used, the intent is the same: we aim to fully involve all generations in the formation of genuine Christian community in order to learn to be followers of Christ.

All-ages learning, as used in this resource, refers to intentional structured learning times with people of all ages. All-ages learning has these characteristics:

- People of all ages come together in an intentional manner to learn. If the group is large, it may be broken down into all-ages units of eight or ten people.

- Story, action and reflection form the basis for all-ages connection. The chosen Bible stories can be understood by all ages.

- The activities are structured in a way that can be done in a group and can be done by all ages.

- It is assumed that people of all ages are engaged in learning for the same reason: everyone, regardless of age, has something important to contribute to the Kingdom of God, although, as people age and mature, they may contribute in more complex and demanding ways.

It should be clarified that all-ages learning is not just the acquisition of knowledge and understanding. Community does not grow and develop unless the learning results in action and reflection. This form of community life is a continuous cycle.

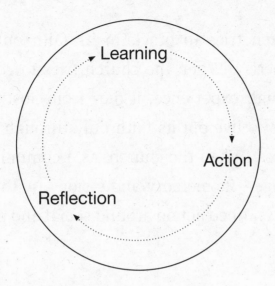

As John Westerhoff reminds us,

> We must act out our faith before we can fully comprehend it. Education requires activism. Religion is not only rational and mystical, it is also practical or moral... We can teach a set of literal beliefs by verbal instruction, but we cannot evolve a living faith. Faith cannot come alive in a person apart from its conceptualization in moments of significant action. Faith cannot be our faith if we only talk about it.[1]

It is not possible to grow a community of wisdom and depth with only one of these components – learning, action, *or* reflection. That is why, in the lessons that follow in Part 2, the activities are just as important as the Bible story. The discussion and reflection is just as important as the service projects. To consistently skip one of these aspects is to hinder the growth of the community.

When the church tries to proclaim its faith only in words, it dies from hypocrisy. When the church tries to communicate its faith only through experience, it dies from abstractness. When the church tries to live out its faith only through actions, it dies from rootlessness. When the church, as a community in history, unites its heritage – its memory and vision – with reflected-upon experience and planned action around social and personal issues, it lives.[2]

Who are the five generations in the church?

What other institution do you know where five generations come together every week – worshipping, drinking juice and coffee, talking, eating, doing important mission work, and learning together what it means to love God and love a neighbour as oneself? The church provides a natural environment for all-ages gatherings. But, as Edward Loper reminds us,

There was a time, not all that long ago, when we did not need to intentionally talk about the relationships between generations. The relationships were plain for all to see. Most [of us] lived in the context of an extended family. Members of several generations lived in a close proximity to one another, knew each other, and supported each other. This is no longer the case.[3]

It is time, once again, to become intentional in building connections among the generations. Few environments or institutions celebrate the mingling of the generations like the church. Certainly, we don't expect it of our schools, medical systems, community clubs, or even businesses. Before thinking about how to set up all-ages learning, it is helpful to look at the component parts of the various age groups of the five generations.

The five generations are sometimes called cohort groups, because the era in which each was born has a profound effect on people. It is not uncommon, for instance, to find that two people born in the same country and in the same year share similar values and outlooks. Understanding some general characteristics of these generations is valuable. However, it is important to remember that these characteristics do not describe *all* the people in the group. In his book *One Church, Four Generations,* Gary McIntosh claims that these broad-stroke generalizations may describe only 75 percent of the people in that era. That means one in four of us will be marching to a different drummer.[4]

Labels used to describe the five generations

These cohort groups have had many names. As a way of describing the broad characteristics of the five generations found in churches in North America, we can use these labels:

- Builders (born prior to 1946)
- Boomers (born between 1946 and 1964)
- Busters or Generation X (born between 1965 and 1983)
- Bridgers or Generation Y (born between 1984 and 2002)
- Unnamed generation (born between 2003 and the present day)[5]

General characteristics of the various generations

Some defining traits of Builders
(born prior to 1946):

- Influenced by World War I, World War II and the Great Depression of the 1930s.
- Large percentage led rural lifestyle.
- Key technologies were cars and radio.
- Personality traits include loyalty, patriotism, respect of tradition (especially family, church, school), hard work, saving, privacy, caution, stability, dependability.
- In religious life, value Bible knowledge and Bible study, Sunday school, emphasis on "foreign" mission.

Some defining traits of Boomers

(born between 1946 and 1964):

- Born in a time of relative affluence.
- Those born later in this era tend to be more politically conservative.
- Formative experiences include civil rights movements, Kennedy administration (in the United States) and the Trudeau era (in Canada), sexual revolution, feminism, Woodstock, Vietnam War.
- Key technologies were television, more efficient cars and highways, airline travel.
- Have highest education levels of any generation up to this time.
- Personality traits included independence, activism, fitness consciousness, questioning of authority, orientation to local activity.
- In religious life, value relationships, commitment to Christ as a personal choice, tolerance of differences, people over programmes.

Some defining traits of Busters/Generation X

(born between 1965 and 1983):

- Formative experiences include Challenger disaster, collapse of Berlin wall, Persian Gulf War, AIDS, Oklahoma City bombing, Clinton administration (in the United States), Much Music generation.
- Key technologies include proliferation of computers, cell phones, fax machines, VCRs.
- Personality traits include value of freedom and flexibility; responsiveness to global issues such as AIDS, world hunger,

homelessness; possible feelings of neglect due to high percentage of divorced and/or working parents; willingness to work; possible rejection of Boomer values; value of practical education.

- In religious life, value family and local causes, having choices and less structure.

Some defining traits of Bridgers/Generation Y

(born between 1984 and 2002):

- Formative experiences include inhabiting an era dominated by "post-modern thinking" where "truth" is inclusive, interactive, complex; high profile of high school violence such as the Columbine and Taber, Alberta, shootings; speed in business world; terrorist attacks in New York on September 11, 2001.
- Defining technology is the Internet.
- Personality traits include entrepreneurialism, technological savvy, neotraditionalism, tolerance, interactiveness, determination to build strong relationships (because many come from divorced families). Many have become used to power as children due to new parenting styles, so may seem demanding.
- In religious life, value holistic experience, enjoy high tech experiences, attempt to grapple with truth.

The unnamed generation

Aren't we lucky? We have a fifth generation present with us in our churches. Wonderful little children and babies born since 2003 who are young enough – mercifully – to have escaped being labelled...so far. This latest generation may not be able to participate in all-ages learning in an active or specific way, but their presence is very much felt: they may be present in their baby-tote; they may need soothing while study proceeds; they may need childcare at nap time.

In our congregation we have a group of older people who have been the Come Join Us club for many decades. One of their recurring themes is, "We're getting older, you know." Last year a young, vibrant couple joined our congregation after immigrating from South Africa. Someone invited them to the Come Join Us club and, surprisingly, they joined in, participating in all the activities. When a baby was born to this young couple, Come Join Us members embraced the baby eagerly, stating quite emphatically that, because the baby had no grandparents, aunts or uncles nearby, they could and would stand in. As they hosted a baby shower for little Daniel, their faces shone with pride, for this was truly "their" baby. What a wonderful example of the powerful influence a small child of the fifth generation can have in an all-ages community.

Can these generations really learn together?

Looking over the characteristics of the generations, we might conclude that there are divisions between them which may seem insurmountable. In observing the generation gap between adult children and their older parents, it is easy to conclude that the adult children may have more in common with their siblings or friends than with their parents. Is it possible for the generations to truly understand each other, let alone learn together?

This is where the church – the community of faith – has an advantage. The things that separate the generations are not nearly as strong as the things that unite. As a group, all generations have a relative openness to God. They acknowledge God's presence and are intentional about seeking to be in the presence of God. All generations acknowledge that the church helps them make meaning of or discern answers to the big "why" questions of life. All generations are aware that faith is not static but keeps changing and evolving. They know that it is not possible to be a Christian without a community. They acknowledge that they aim to live as Jesus did and follow his teachings. They understand that there are many ways to experience truth – through scripture, through reason, through tradition, through experience.[6]

It is these uniting elements that declare, "Yes! We can learn together, because we share a world view that has a certain orientation. The things that unite us are greater than the things that divide." Ultimately, the intergenerational learning group wants not just to learn *about* God, but to *know* God, to express and receive love, and "to hold tenderly the mystery of that encounter."[7]

Why do all-ages learning?

There are lots of advantages to learning together in all-ages groups.

We learn from each other, regardless of age

We know that, in this five-generation community, we do not teach Christianity like we teach math or computer skills. The learning that we do in the church is more *caught* than *taught*. Yes, we want to know the Bible stories *and* the type of literature in the Bible *and* how we might interpret difficult passages *and* where to find sources of comfort and guidance. But more important than biblical knowledge is the desire for a growing, deepening, and broadening experience with the Bible. Why do people continue to read and study the Bible? How does the story of the Good Samaritan speak to my life? How will I live my life differently because of what I read in the Bible? These are hard things to figure out, but are made easier when the community struggles with them together.

Recently, I was working with a group of children and adults learning about HIV/AIDS in Africa. Even though I was the teacher, I learned something important from a young girl. During our study, we wore African clothes and ate nsima and masamba. We worked on a model African village. We did puzzles and read stories about children who were orphans because of AIDS. On the third week of our study, Ashleigh came up to me and put her hands on her hips. "Mrs. Henderson," she said firmly, "We have simply *got* to stop talking about AIDS." She paused, then continued, "And *do* something about it." The other adults and I looked at each other. Of course! Ashleigh was right. With such a serious issue, we *had* to take action. And, because of the fierce reminder of a child, that is exactly what we did. All-ages learning is a two-way street. Ashleigh learned the important facts about AIDS from her adult teachers, but from Ashleigh we adults learned that we needed to act. We all learn from each other.

We need the perspective that various generations bring

Have you ever visited a church where there is only one generation – all the members are seniors, or it is a "targeted" church where all the members are teens? How much richer is a church community where people of all ages are encouraged to be in full membership.

Suppose, for instance, in an all-ages class, four generations came together before Christmas to study peace. An eight-year-old, a 28-year-old, a 50-year-old, and an 82-year-old all read together from Isaiah:

> They shall beat their swords into plowshares,
> and their spears into pruning hooks;
> nation shall not lift up sword against nation,
> neither shall they learn war any more (Isaiah 2:4).

After everyone has read this passage, the group leader asks, "What do you know about war?" The eight-year-old tells about seeing news coverage of the Iraqi war on television. The 28-year-old tells about hearing war stories from her grandfather. The 50-year-old tells about seeing photos of a burning child running down a street during the Vietnam War. And the 82-year-old tells about serving in the navy in World War II. Who will have the "right" perspective on this passage? Obviously, not one person. But the various perspectives of all the generations will add to the richness of the study. We might say that they make up a multiple-meaning system. The 82-year-old may remind the group that understanding and depth of reason comes from longevity. The 50-year-old may remind the group that a new world lens is needed to avoid turning a volatile Middle East situation into a powder keg. The 28-year-old may remind the group that it is important to keep idealism alive so the world is not overcome with hopelessness. And the child, in her youthful openness, may remind all the adults of the need for each generation to learn again the ways of peace. All will learn from each other.

A congregation is like an extended family

There is a children's chorus that says

> I am the church. You are the church. We are the church together.
> All of God's children, all around the world, yes, we're the church together.

> The church is not a building. The church is not a steeple.
> The church is not a resting place. The church is the people!

The church is much more than a structure where people attend worship, listen to a sermon, and sing hymns on Sunday morning. It is the community of people – a *particular* people. This community can gather in a cathedral, a living room, a camp cabin, a college dorm. God's people are a particular lot. They truly believe that, where two or three are gathered together, they are like a big family and God is in their midst.

In 2 Timothy 1:1–7, there is a wonderful all-ages family – Timothy; his mother, Eunice; and his grandmother, Lois. We don't know why Timothy is growing up in a family where there is no father, but it is a story that many young people today can identify with. Lois and Eunice had a great influence on young Timothy, and so does the writer of the letter.[8] He says that Timothy is constantly in his prayers, that he remembers Timothy's tears when they were last together, and he longs to see Timothy again so he might be filled with joy. The writer is not only extremely fond of young Timothy, but he commends Timothy's grandmother, Lois, and his mother, Eunice, for raising him as a Christian.

The Search Institute, a religious research organization in the United States, did a survey of thousands of Christian teens, asking them, "Who was the person most influential in leading you to become a person of faith?"[9] They generated a long list, but at the top of the list was Mother. Number two was Father. Close behind was Grandmother. The story of Timothy is a wonderful reminder that family, extended family, and older mentors are the primary means by which faith develops.

In the church, we simulate an extended family by gathering in small groups. These small intergenerational groups are a source of support and nurture to each other. As one minister said, "Everyone – adult and child – must have the opportunity to share his or her insights with others. It's in the sharing at the end that we participate in one another's growth."[10] Sometimes older people comment on how encouraging it is to see children, youth and younger adults take a keen interest in the church and the Bible. It is just as encouraging for young people to see seniors who have trusted in God all their lives and continue to follow Jesus. The sense of extended family in the community of believers is an encouragement to all.

All-ages learning transmits Christianity from generation to generation

In their book *Generation to Generation*, John Westerhoff, a theologian, and Gwen Kennedy Neville, an anthropologist, point out how religion and culture are transmitted from parents to children in religious-cultural communities. This process involves stories, people, experiences, and a shared outlook on the world. Westherhoff and Neville cite, for instance, the fact that many families return for a summer camping experience in the same location. There, on a yearly basis, they meet others who share similar values and beliefs. These experiences provide continuity and stability. In his little book *Building an Intergenerational Church*, Edward A. Loper explains that the job of family is to transmit the family and cultural values from one generation to another while keeping the children safe.[11]

In the church, we aim to consciously transmit our Christian story from generation to generation. We pass on what it means to be moral and productive members of society, and we model what it means to be faithful followers of Christ. We teach children and youth to love worship and participate in the sacraments. This is an enormous job

– one that is much bigger than parents can do alone. For help, we rely on "extended family" – other members of the church community.

The time is right for all-ages learning

Throughout history, people have learned together. Youth have learned how to cut trees from their fathers and grandfathers. Children have learned how to knead bread from their aunts, mothers and grandmothers. Children learned to milk a cow under the tutelage of a parent or a hired hand. Today, even though many of these natural times to learn are less obvious, generations are still looking for activities to do together.

A church I know performed an unintentional experiment. Wanting to offer more options to the parents and grandparents who brought small children to church, the congregation offered two choices: a beautiful, well-equipped, staffed nursery *and* an informal area at the back of the sanctuary where the adults could sit in rocking chairs and the children could enjoy soft toys and books. Interestingly, about half the parents and grandparents took their children to the nursery (perhaps they needed quiet reflection time) while the other half stayed with their children in the worship service.

Many parents and grandparents are opting for time with their children and grandchildren. Many adults in the church grew up learning in age-segregated classes. Now work, school and child care keep the generations separate all week. Busy parents see too little of their children, and equally busy grandparents desire to spend more time – and quality time – with children and youth. They want to be together at church.

It is not only parents and grandparents who are looking for more quality and interactive time with youth. Others in the congregation – singles, adults far from their own grandchildren, youth who love babysitting, young couples expecting their first child – enjoy and welcome time to learn in all-ages groups. The time is right for all-ages learning.

All-ages learning can heal

Generational healing can be a natural by-product of learning together. It can bring reconciliation to the generations. It helps generations realize that, while they may have different views and values and may understand faith differently, they are not wrong. They are simply different.

One evening, I was invited to do a Christian education workshop in a Hungarian church. All members were relatively new to the country, having arrived after the Hungarian Revolution in 1956. To my surprise and (I have to admit) dismay, when I arrived with my carefully prepared workshop, I discovered a multi-age group of about 25 people – children, youth, young adults, middle adults, and seniors. I could see that my workshop plan wasn't going to work. But what should I do in its place?

I had planned a connecting exercise with a ball of yarn. As the first person held on to the end of the ball of yarn, she tossed the ball to someone across the circle because she wanted to hear an answer to a question I had posed. My first question was, "When did you first learn about God?" My second question was, "Where did you live when you were eight years old?" To my amazement, people refused to stop playing this game. They added questions of their own, calling out, "I want to hear where Janos met his wife," and "I want to know where people hid during the war." The young were curious about the old who had lived through both the second world war and the violent Hungarian Revolution. The old were suddenly sympathetic to the middle adults who struggled to make their way in a new culture, language, and job in North America. The children understood, perhaps for the first time, how the older generations struggled with a language that they had to learn as adults. This all-ages conversation was a time of bridging, healing, reconciliation, and new understanding.

All-ages learning can challenge

Sometimes, in the Christian community, we need others to hold us accountable. We *intend* to do some useful Christian activity, but time runs out. We *mean* to engage in some challenging action, but, alone, we lose our courage. All-ages groups can work together to motivate each other in Christian service.

Years ago, a friend told me a story about a teacher in India. When visitors came to the school, they always commented on the discipline and inner strength of the children. "How," they asked, "have you managed to instil this so well in your students?" The teacher answered that she was not sure. Then she added thoughtfully, "It might be our Friday afternoons…" Although the students were among the most economically deprived in the region, they set aside each Friday afternoon to do "one challenging thing." Sometimes, with their teacher's help, the children gave away a prized possession to someone who was just as poor as they were. Sometimes, with their teacher's help, they hoed vegetables under the hot sun for someone who was sick. Sometimes, with their teacher's help, they washed clothes for a new mother. What a wonderful story of how many challenging things children can do to make a difference in the world... *if* caring adults are willing to do it with them. These are the kinds of experiences that can and do evolve when all ages learn together.

All-ages learning is playful

Somehow, in the church, we have come to think of education and learning as terribly serious business. Sometimes it is, but how much more enjoyable learning is when it is playful. It is fun for seniors to learn to dance an Israeli circle dance with teens. It is fun for churches to have a surprise visit from a clown who mimes a parable. James White tells of a wonderful surprise when two lions (Golden Retrievers with black cardboard manes) came down the sanctuary aisle. And he recalls, with amusement and a touch of horror, the day the sprinklers came on in the courtyard as Elijah's enacted prophecy of rain came true! He tells of a church which had a "central character" as part of the unit. This person, who dressed and acted in character – Elijah, St. Andrew, Dr. Spock, Herbert the Snail, the Wizard of Oz – provided regular fun for the learners.

In the course of planning for churches, it is helpful to think that programmes and activities should have at least one of these purposes:

Worship   Learning/education

Service/Mission   Fellowship/fun

When an activity or programme combines two or more of these elements, it becomes powerful. For instance, the congregation of St. Andrews Presbyterian Church in Newmarket, Ontario, offers a programme called "Boarding House Ministries," where teams of six people go to a Boarding House which is home to adults suffering from mental illness. This has been a powerful ministry, because it combines all four elements – a worship time, a focused service to support and encourage those with mental illnesses, lots of fun and laughter (they even developed their own secret code which means "wonderful joke"), and opportunities for Bible study and learning life skills.

Similarly, in the same congregation, the pre-schoolers participate in a programme called *Young Children and Worship.* Although they are only ages three to five, the children participate fully in a sensate worship and a strong educational time. Because it combines two of the four elements, this pre-school programme is strong.

In Part 2 of this resource, the all-ages sessions are intentional about integrating learning, fun, and service. By including a moment of worship, all four elements of a strong programme are present in the all-ages experiences.

How do we do all-ages learning?

There are two ways of being intentional about building links among the generations. Church leaders can intentionally add an all-ages component into already existing church events. Or congregations can plan intentionally structured programmes – a specific unit of learning, often with a seasonal theme.

Intentional integration

Intentional integration capitalizes on normal congregational patterns. It is consciousness raising. Church leaders simply watch, over and over, for ways to make links between the generations in the everyday events of the congregation. For instance, if your congregation has a potluck meal once a month, add to the tables some conversation cards that ask people to find someone from another generation to talk to about something specific. If children and their parents attend a yearly spirituality retreat, involve other generations (youth, middle, and senior adults) by asking for prayer partners or by inviting the other generations to prepare snacks or crafts. When you host a confirmation class for youth, involve other generations by recruiting mentors or running the class as a youth-parent event. Once you have begun looking at church life through an all-ages lens, the possibilities are endless.

Below is a list of possible existing programmes where all-ages integration might happen:

- camps
- dinners
- evangelism events
- picnics
- new member gatherings
- outreach projects
- stewardship events
- meetings
- staff work (e.g. the church secretary can show children and seniors how to run the copier or the custodian can involve others in care of the building)

Structured programmes

In his book *Intergenerational Religious Education*, James White compares churches to sailing ships.[12] A ship may have many sails, but not all can or should be raised at once. It is necessary and important to set priorities. Choose the all-ages programme or event that is important for the community at a particular time. Every congregation can structure learning programmes such as an all-ages Sunday school, a retreat, or a seasonal event. Part 2 of this resource offers one way to do this – by providing class activities in five-week units. Remember, though, that while programming is important, it will not do the whole job. Having an all-ages mindset ensures that all-ages links are continual.

Below is a list of possible milieus for structured programmes:

- an intergenerational discussion programme
- a one-time event for a school holiday

- the usual Sunday school time
- an after-worship programme
- Sunday or weeknight supper
- Vacation Bible School combined with a barbeque
- an add-on programme to an existing men's or women's fellowship
- a one-time congregational event called something like "Coffee, Coke, and Cake"
- a short-term Sunday school class
- one-on-one ministries such as a "Grandfriends" programme or pen pal exchanges
- prayer partnerships
- visitation programmes for frail seniors
- oral histories gathered by children and youth from older people
- intergenerational church care programmes (combined child care and day-away programmes for seniors)
- "Rocking Chair" ministry – inviting seniors to rock small children in the nursery
- intergenerational storytellers who visit children's classes
- mentors for new Christians or youth
- all-ages game or video night
- "Senior Prom" where youth invite a senior to the dance
- Seniors providing child care so parents can work at a Habitat for Humanity site
- an intergenerational retreat
- a worship-education programme such as an intergenerational Holy Week walk

Characteristics of all-ages learning

The format you choose for delivering an all-ages learning programme can vary widely. The format that's right for each church will depend on key factors such as the size of the congregation, the amount of available space on a given day, and the congregational priorities.

Regardless of the format or model that is chosen, it is important to incorporate these elements into the activity:

- **Movement** – Use space-to-space movement or carpet-to-table movement. Even older learners need fresh starts in a variety of settings. When the body moves, the brain works.

- **Use of the senses** – Go on trust walks, use musical instruments, read poetry, listen to music from other countries, listen to a recording of birds chirping, smell bread baking, taste a Seder meal, feel the rough canvas of Abraham and Sarah's travelling tent.

- **Sensitivity to life-development abilities** – Know what people are capable of doing at various stages of life. Don't expect an eight-year-old, for instance, to read the New Revised Standard Version of the Bible, which is written at a Grade 8 reading level. Don't expect the seniors in your group to sit on the floor. Look for commonalities in all the age groups.

Steps to follow in beginning all-ages learning

1. Set goals. What do you want to see happen as a result of all-ages learning? Will there be more awareness of the importance of cross-generational activity in the congregation? Are you trying

to address a logistics problem, such as parents needing to drive their children to Sunday school at another time? Are you looking for a new approach to a tired Sunday school? Is it a way to coax adults into an educational programme? Is it a way to provide support across generations? Goals help planners define why they might use all-ages learning in a specific context.

2. Enlist the support of the minister and other key leaders. Explain clearly to the minister of your congregation what all-ages learning is and why you would like to use it. Ask to make a presentation to the governing body of your congregation. They will want to hear the goals of your programme, and know if there are financial needs.

3. Obtain the support of lay leaders. Prior to starting all-ages programmes, it is helpful to ask a group of lay leaders for initial help. Explain to them that, as the all-ages events proceed, leadership will begin to come from within the groups. Confident Sunday school teachers, or leaders of a youth group, or adult fellowship group can be helpful in providing leadership in the initial stages of your programme.

4. Help the congregation see the opportunities and the needs. It is important to take time to let programmes build. Often it takes as long as 12 months to create awareness before new changes or strategies can be implemented. Communication about the programme can take many forms – e-mail messages, bulletin

announcements, short announcements in worship, requests for prayer. Include your ideas of how all-ages learning will take place, the biblical foundation for doing it, your vision for this new aspect of ministry, and why you need prayer to sustain and guide you. As you are considering or establishing an all-ages programme, specifically invite some members of your congregation to pray for you as the idea is taking shape.

5. Build on the past. As you promote and advertise all-ages learning, you might use words like this:

In the olden days, children and youth worked alongside adults to learn the ropes. Our all-ages class builds on this way of learning. If you would like to learn the great truths of Christianity with people of all ages, join us on...

Or,

Remember who first taught you the Christian faith? Was it your mother? father? grandparent? The Christian faith is more caught than taught. If you would like to be part of catching and teaching the faith in an all-ages group, join us on...

Or,

Adults...do you miss children and youth in your life? Join our all-ages class and connect with young people as you learn together.

6. You may choose to begin in a small, informal way. Instead of starting with a full-fledged Sunday school programme, offer a small, informal all-ages event such as a 24-hour retreat or an evening event with barbecue or potluck meal.

7. Choose activities and stories that help generations understand each other, and that all generations can do easily. When choosing activities and stories, ask repeatedly, "Can this activity be done by all ages? Is this story appropriate for all ages?" For instance, the game Twister may be fun for children, youth and young adults, but it is difficult for seniors. The story of Joshua bringing down the walls of Jericho may seem appropriate for all ages until you read the part where Joshua and his band of believers slaughter all the inhabitants and animals in the city. How would you explain this to a child?

8. Finally, set up all-ages planning groups. As all-ages learning proceeds, it is crucial that the leadership team develops into an all-ages group. At a minimum, assemble an implementation team of two people with representatives from older and younger generations. Because the oldest generation (Builders) tends to assume much church leadership, it is important to be intentional about encouraging Boomers and Busters, assisted by Bridgers, to take leadership.

Leadership consideration in all-ages groups

The particular leadership role of adults

Although leadership can and should be shared by representatives from all the generations, it is likely that the impetus for leadership will come from two or three motivated adults who believe strongly in the benefits of all-ages events. Use the following strategies for conducting successful intergenerational meetings.[13]

1. Be creative and sensitive about meeting times, places, and transportation.

2. Understand the needs of participants. Will they arrive hungry? Will they need a reminder of the meeting? Will they need calendars to schedule the next meeting?

3. Try to have all four or five generations present at the meeting. Keep all the generations in mind as you plan the activity choices. Expect everyone to be an active participant.

4. Greet people the minute they walk in. This lets people know they are in the right place. Provide something for people to do right away, so they do not sit around waiting for others to arrive.

5. Acknowledge to the group that intergenerational learning may be a new experience for many people, and that you are all learning together how to study in all-ages groups.

6. Start with a check-in or icebreaker. This helps people feel more comfortable and connected at the beginning of a meeting.

7. Talk about language issues. Will everyone be called by first names? Do children object to being called "kids"?

8. Value the people who show up. Avoid saying, "I'm sorry there aren't more people here today." Assume instead that the people who come are the right people.

9. Give each participant – regardless of age – an opportunity to talk.

10. Have in mind some system for allowing everyone to speak, and for discouraging a person who speaks too often. You may, for instance, pass a talking stick around a circle. Only the person holding the talking stick speaks. If the person does not wish to speak, the stick may be passed to a neighbour.

11. If the energy level in the room drops, invite people to turn to a neighbour and talk in pairs.

12. Frequently break into small groups. People are more inclined to speak in smaller groups.

13. It is important to plan and *do* activities. Be sure to incorporate the experience and knowledge from all generations. For instance, older people may be able to share their love of woodworking, sewing, or knitting. Younger people may be able to share their computer skills, reading, or art skills.

14. Use brainstorming. This helps people generate a wide variety of creative ideas, if they know their ideas won't be judged.

15. If decisions must be made, use consensus rather than voting. Ask the group, "Can everyone live with this?" If someone cannot, think about ways to compromise.

16. Close the meeting time with a brief affirmation or positive comment.

Putting together a leadership team

Regardless of whether you do structured programming or unstructured consciousness-raising within the congregation, it is important to have a small leadership team that cares deeply about all-ages learning. This team might include the minister, one or two church leaders, a child, and a youth. Two or three meetings may be necessary to think through how all-ages learning can best be done in your context.

Resources for all-ages learning

In addition to the suggested resources listed in the session plans in Part 2, it is helpful to think of things that all generations have in common. Make use of the following resources:

- **People** – Invite guests who work in a specific area. Are you studying the story of the rich young ruler? Invite a bank manager and ask him/her to speak about attitudes people have towards money.

- **Books** – Many children's story books have strong appeal across generations.[14] Use art books, coffee table books with beautiful photos, picture Bible dictionaries, etc.

- **Internet** – Even most seniors use the internet. If you have a computer in your meeting space, use it for research.

- **Phone** – Simulate a "call" to ask God a question. Actually call a mission staff person overseas.

- **Items that express a world view** – These can be globes, atlases, satellite photos. You might, for instance, after telling a Bible story, spin a globe and ask participants to imagine that they are in southern Africa. How would they hear that story if they lived there?

- **TV/video/DVD** – Versions of many common Bible stories can be found in this format.

Endnotes

1   John H. Westerhoff III and Gwen Kennedy Neville, *Generation to Generation* (Pilgrim Press, 1974), 86.

2   Ibid., 155.

3   Edward A. Loper, *Building an Intergenerational Church* (Louisville: Geneva Press, 1999), 3.

4   Gary McIntosh writes within the context of the United States of America, so these descriptions may, in fact, be primarily descriptive only of Americans. Within Canada, demographer Michael Adams has written a similar book about generational differences entitled *Sex in the Snow* (Penguin Canada, 1997). No doubt, other countries have sociologists who have noted generational group characteristics for their context.

5   As this generation grows and is shaped by the cultural values in which it lives, it, too, will acquire a label.

6   These "four ways of knowing" came from the work of John Wesley, 1703–1791.

7   Daniel O. Aleshire, Faith Care: Ministering to All God's People Through the Ages of Life (Westminster Press, 1988), 50.

8   Bible scholars agree that, although this letter states that it is written by Paul, the unique style of the letter indicates that it was probably written by one of Paul's many helpers or travelling companions. This was a common practice 2,000 years ago: if you were a disciple of a particular person, you had tacit permission to write in that person's name.

9   1998, Youth and Family Institute of Augsburg College, Campus Box 70, 2211 Riverside Avenue, Minneapolis, MN 55454-1351.

10 James W. White, *Intergenerational Religious Education* (Religious Education Press, 1988), 205.

11 Loper, *Building an Intergenerational Church*, 5.

12 James W. White, *Intergenerational Religious Education* (Religious Education Press, 1988), 194.

13 These strategies were adapted from *Working Shoulder to Shoulder*, by Deborah Fisher (Search Institute, 2004).

14 Good examples are Robert Munsch's *Love you Forever* (Firefly Books, 1995) and *Something from Nothing* by Phoebe Gilman (Scholastic, Canada, 1994). Both have strong intergenerational themes.

PART 2

Four units of lessons for all-ages groups

Preparing to use the lessons

Ways to use this resource

There are many ways to use the sessions in *Learning God's Stories Together*:

- As a regular Sunday school programme
- At an intergenerational retreat
- In a home school setting
- As a family Bible study
- In a regular devotional time
- Where regular worship attendance is impossible for families because of shift work or Sunday retail

The possibilities are endless.

How the sessions are organized

Each of the 20 story sessions consists of four parts:

1. Gathering to hear the story
2. Telling and talking about the story
3. Exploring the story
4. Making the story part of your life

Before you begin

It is very important that you round up some things.

1. All the stories in the sessions are taken from *The Family Story Bible*, by Ralph Milton (Northstone, 1996). This book is available from most major denominational bookstores, or from the publisher at 1.800.663.2775 or woodlakebooks.com. All the biblical references are given as well, so if you are unable to locate the book, it is possible to use the Bible. However, the author of *The Family Story Bible*, Ralph Milton, tells the biblical story through an imaginative and child-sensitive lens. In addition, the soft and gentle art of Margaret Kyle appeals to children, youth, and adults alike.

2. All the music suggestions are from *LifeSongs* (Augsburg Fortress, 1999). Since all the song suggestions are quite specific to the story and are short and easy for children to learn, it is strongly suggested that you purchase this songbook. Check with your denominational bookstore.

3. Many of the exploration activities make use of simple things – magazines, clay, scissors, pipe cleaners, scarves or shirts (for drama), crayons, markers, paper, glue, and tape. Put together a basic craft box that can be the foundation for the exploration activities. This will save a lot of rounding up each session.

Serving food

It is always wonderful to share a snack together. Sharing food is a bonding and friendly experience. If you are a family group, you may do these studies after a family meal, but if you do them in the afternoon or morning, it is a good idea to have cookies, fruit, tea, or milk ready. The same is true if you are doing this study with a church group. Many of the sessions suggest specific foods that go well with the story.

Who will lead the sessions?

It is possible, in a church setting, that various families will take leadership for a story session. But you may need to recruit an experienced leader to begin, especially if this is a new venture in your congregation.

In a home setting, it is likely that a parent will need to take leadership to begin *Learning God's Stories Together*. But, in time, an older child or teen may organize a story session. It is important to give children and youth the opportunity to develop their leadership skills in a safe, supportive environment.

Are the activities suggested too child-focused?

Some adults reading this resource may worry that the storybook and suggested activities may have more appeal to children than to teens and adults. However, it has been the tested experience of the authors that when people intentionally come together in intergenerational groups, adults enjoy working alongside the children and may even rediscover a child-like *joie de vivre*. Adults and teens have many opportunities to learn challenging things with their peer groups. *Learning God's Stories Together*, however, provides a setting for rediscovering what multigenerational interactions can teach us.

Unit A

Superheroes of the Faith

This unit explores the idea of biblical superheroes using these stories:

Abraham and Sarah
begin a journey
(*The Family Story Bible*, p. 28)

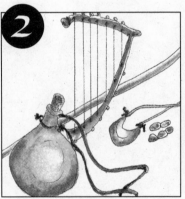

David takes a brave stand
(*The Family Story Bible*, p. 109)

Esther saves her people
(*The Family Story Bible*, p. 126)

Martha struggles
and learns
(*The Family Story Bible*, p. 222)

The boy who shares
his meal
(*The Family Story Bible*, p. 202)

Session 1

Abraham and Sarah begin a journey

Session focus

Abraham and Sarah don't know where they are going, but God makes a promise to lead them.

Gathering to hear the story

Before the session, gather together road maps, atlases, or globes. As people of different ages gather, look over the maps and atlases. Invite each person to show others one place he or she has travelled or would like to travel. Look up your hometown. Find the place to which you have travelled that is farthest from your home.

Telling and talking about the story

Explain that your group will be looking at superheroes of the Bible. Today's story is about two superheroes who went on a long trip, even though they had no map to guide them. Read the story "Abraham and Sarah Begin a Journey," from *The Family Story Bible*, p. 28. (Based on Genesis 12, 13:14–18.)

To talk about the story, use questions like these:

- Why do you think Abram and Sarai changed their names to Abraham and Sarah?
- Describe what would be hard about going on a trip like Abraham and Sarah's?
- What made it difficult for Abraham and Sarah to keep believing God's promise?
- Do you remember a time when you thought God made a promise to you?

Exploring the story

There are many ways to explore this story. Below are some suggestions. Prepare at least two activities, so that people can choose the one that most interests them.

- **Drama:** Play charades. Act out people or animals in this story and have others guess who or what you are.

- **Art:** Make a scrapbook that continues all through this unit. Draw or paint a picture of Abraham and Sarah. (At the end of the unit, the last story in your book can be a page about you.)

- **Sculpture:** Using modelling clay, create a sculpture of your favourite hero (Abraham or Sarah) from this story.

- **Creative writing:** Make a list of the characteristics of a hero.

- **Music:** Learn together and sing the song "Fear not for tomorrow," #161, *LifeSongs*.

- **Food:** Talk about the food that might be used on a camping trip. Prepare and serve pancakes (pretending that the electric fry pan is a campfire). Or mix together and enjoy a travelling food like "gorp" (a mixture of nuts, sunflower seeds, raisins, dried fruit).

- **Maps and patterns**: Find a map of the Middle East (c. 2000 BCE). Locate Haran, Ai, Negev, Egypt. Estimate the distance from Haran to Egypt. How far would Abraham and Sarah's trip be? How far would you have to walk from your house to go the same distance?

- **Serving others**: Make travel aid kits. Think about small items that might be needed by modern day travellers. Gather them together and put them into an envelope labelled "Travel Aid Kit." You might include a safety pin, a needle and some thread, bandage(s), tissues, a stick of gum, pen or pencil, small note pad, elastic band, 25-cent coin, paper clip, etc.

Making the story part of your life

If you have chosen to make travel aid kits, discuss to whom you might give them.

Ask participants what they have learned from the Bible hero today. If someone says that she admired Abraham and Sarah for their courage, say something like this: "Then I hope you will find courage this week in your play and work." Using a marker, write "courage" on the back of the person's hand. In this way, the person can take "courage" into her body and life. Do this for each person, using whatever key word is mentioned (courage, openness, etc.).

Close with a circle prayer. Everyone holds hands, and the leader invites the group to thank God for elements from the story – courage, adventure, family. If someone does not wish to pray aloud, he or she simply squeezes the hand of the next person, and that person continues.

Session 2
David takes a brave stand

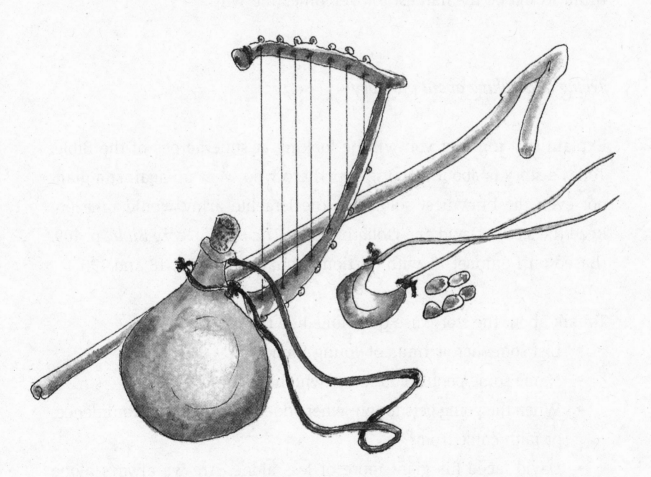

> **Session focus**
>
> David is just a boy, a young shepherd facing a giant, but he knows God is with him.

Gathering to hear the story

Before you gather, pull pictures of movie villains from magazines or the Internet. Invite participants to find someone of a different age and, in pairs, look over the pictures. Ask them to discuss which villain they think would be the hardest to overcome, and why.

Telling and talking about the story

Explain that together you will be looking at superheroes of the Bible. Today's story is about a young superhero who went up against a giant not even the brawniest soldier in the Israelite army would take on. Read the story "David and Goliath," from *The Family Story Bible,* p. 109. (Based on 1 Samuel 17, with portions from chapters 16, 18 and 19.)

To talk about the story, use questions like these:
- List some heroic traits of young David.
- Name some people you know who have these traits.
- When the going gets tough, where does your courage, confidence, or faith come from?
- David faced his giant more or less alone. Are we always alone facing our giants? Name some important people in your support circle.

Exploring the story

There are many ways to explore this story. Below are some suggestions. Prepare at least two activities, so that people can choose the one that most interests them.

- **Drama:** Re-enact the story of David and Goliath.
- **Art:** If you have begun a scrapbook from session one, add a picture of David to your scrapbook.
- **Sculpture**: Create a papier mâché sculpture of David, or Abraham and Sarah (from the previous session). To make papier mâché, you will need newspaper and a large bowl of flour paste (flour mixed with water). Dip strips of newspaper into the flour paste and shape into a person, sheep or wolf. For the main body of the sculpture, wad a large sheet of newspaper into the core shape of the object. Then continue to add smaller strips to create features like arms, legs, heads, tails. Set aside to dry completely (two or three days). When it is dry, you may paint it.
- **Creative writing**: Make a list of the characteristics of a hero. If you began a list last session, add to it. The first letter of each word can be a puffy balloon letter. Colour the puffy letter according to what you imagine is appropriate for the word; i.e., what colour do you think courage is?
- **Music:** Sing "Jesus, shepherd us," #157, *LifeSongs*.
- **Food:** Make "giant" chocolate chip cookies. Soak 3 cups (750 ml) of rolled oats in 1 cup (250 ml) of milk for at least ten minutes. Sift together 2 cups (500 ml) all-purpose flour, 1 teaspoon (5 ml) baking soda, and 1 teaspoon (5 ml) salt. Set aside. Cream together 1 cup (250 ml) margarine, 1 cup (250 ml) packed brown sugar,

and 1/2 cup (125 ml) white sugar. Stir in 2 eggs and 1 teaspoon (5 ml) vanilla extract. Add the sifted ingredients and mix well. Stir in the oat mixture and 1 cup (250 ml) semisweet chocolate chips. Drop the dough by heaping spoonfuls onto oiled cookie sheets. Spread the dough together so two or three spoonfuls make a giant cookie. Bake for 12 to 15 minutes in a preheated 350°F (180°C) oven, until the cookies are golden brown. Cool on baking sheets or remove them to cool on wire racks.

- **Maps and patterns:** If possible, find pictures of biblical shepherds. How do you imagine their life? Many shepherds had sheepfolds to keep the sheep safe at night. Can you find a picture of a sheepfold? Find a picture of a modern-day shepherd. How has a shepherd's life changed? How has it stayed the same?

- **Serving others:** Being a shepherd is like being a caregiver. Think of a particular way you can be a caregiver for someone this week – helping a small child, a senior, or a person who needs help crossing a street.

Making the story part of your life

If you made giant cookies, decide with whom you might share them.

Ask group members what they have learned from the David story. Invite people to share, but it is not necessary that everyone say something aloud.

Close with a circle prayer. Everyone holds hands, and the leader invites the group to thank God for elements from the story – fearlessness, faith, leadership. If someone does not wish to pray aloud, he or she simply squeezes the hand of the next person, and that person continues.

Session 3
Esther saves her people

Session focus

An outsider chosen to be queen finds a way to stand up to the king and save her people.

Gathering to hear the story

From a local newspaper, find pictures of ordinary people who have done something special. Invite participants to look over the pictures and articles with someone of a different age and discuss what would make an ordinary member of the community do a brave thing like that.

Telling and talking about the story

Explain that you will continue to look at superheroes of the Bible. Today's story is about a young Hebrew woman, Esther, who was chosen to be queen to the king of Persia. She has to talk back to the king in order to save her people. Talking back would have been an amazing thing for a woman to do in the ancient Middle East. Women were considered second class citizens. In addition, at that time, kings were deemed to be appointed by God or "the gods," so to talk back to a king would be like sassing God. Read the story "Esther saves her people," from *The Family Story Bible*, p. 126. (Based on Esther 2.)

To talk about the story, use questions like these:
- Can you name another story where an ordinary person saves the day?
- Do you think you would be ready for such a challenge?
- How does Esther prepare herself for her little chat with the king?
- How would you prepare yourself?

Exploring the story

There are many ways to explore this story. Below are some suggestions. Prepare at least two activities, so that people can choose the one that most interests them.

- **Drama:** Create a slide show or photo display. Act out scenes from Esther's story and take pictures with a digital camera (for a slide show) or a disposable camera (for a photo display). Here is a list of shots to take:

   1. The king is introduced to Esther.

   2. Haman is scowling.

   3. Haman and the king are talking. Haman is making a hand-across-throat gesture. The king is nodding.

   4. Mordecai is writing a letter.

   5. Esther is reading a letter, shaking her head, no.

   6. Esther has a mixing bowl.

   7. The king is at the table with dirty dishes, reading a book.

   8. Esther is chatting with the king, who is still holding the book; the king is looking shocked at her news.

   9. The king is shouting at Haman.

   10. Esther, Mordecai, and the king are smiling at each other.

- **Art:** If you have been making a scrapbook, add a picture of Esther, or, alternatively, you may hand paint a tile with a key verse from Esther ("If you keep silence at such a time as this..." 4:14). You will need unpainted tiles from a home supply store, tile paints and brushes, aprons or smocks, old newspapers, paper towelling. Younger participants may simply paint a picture of Esther rather than add the suggested scripture verse.

- **Sculpture:** Using homemade play dough, shape the figures in this story. To make play dough, combine 2 cups (500 ml) flour and 1 cup (250 ml) salt. Add 1 cup (250 ml) water. Add a few drops of oil to keep the mixture from drying out. If desired, add food colouring to the water. Knead for a few minutes and store in a tightly closed plastic container until ready to use.

- **Creative writing:** Write a haiku using the theme "hero." A haiku is a Japanese poem that has three lines. The first line has five syllables, the second line has seven, and the third line has five. Here is an example:

  Esther was so brave.

  She saved her people, the Jews.

  Awesome brave woman.

- **Music:** Sing "Fear not for tomorrow," #161, *LifeSongs.*

- **Food:** Make a party platter of vegetables and dip to highlight the celebrating and feasting aspect of this story. Prepare carrots, celery, broccoli, mushrooms, cherry tomatoes, and whatever else you like. To make an easy hummus dip, sauté 2 cloves of garlic, peeled and crushed, in 2 tablespoons (30 ml) of olive oil for three minutes. In a blender put 1 can garbanzo beans (chick peas), drained, and 1 teaspoon (5 ml) of the reserved bean liquid. Process until smooth. If too thick, add a little of the reserved bean liquid. Pour into a bowl. Stir in the cooked garlic, 1 tablespoon (15 ml) of sesame seeds, salt and pepper to taste. Chill in the refrigerator until serving.

- **Maps and patterns:** Using the list of shots under Drama as a guide, draw the scenes from the story on index cards. Shuffle them. Then put them in order on a rope, attaching each with a clothes pin.

- **Serving others:** Talk about one hard thing that will come up in your week ahead. How will you serve others as Esther did?

Making the story part of your life

Invite people to share one thing they have learned from Esther's story. If someone says that he admired Esther for her spunk, respond with something like this: "I hope you will find spunk like hers in your life this week."

Close with a circle prayer. Everyone holds hands, and the leader invites the group to thank God for elements from the story – courage, faith, leadership. If someone does not wish to pray aloud, he or she simply squeezes the hand of the next person, and that person continues.

Session 4
Martha struggles
and learns

Session focus

Martha struggles with how to be hospitable to Jesus, and she learns something important about food.

Gathering to hear the story

Before people gather, pull pictures of terrific looking meals or desserts from magazines or newspaper flyers. Ask each person to find someone who is a different age and look over the pictures. Invite them to talk about their favourite foods.

Telling and talking about the story

Explain that the group will continue to look at superheroes of the Bible. Read the story "Martha learns about food," from *The Family Story Bible*, p. 222. (Based on Luke 10:38–42.)

To talk about the story, use questions like these:

- In what way does Martha seem like a hero to you?
- Whenever we meet Martha in the Bible, she seems feisty. Why do you think Jesus liked this kind of friend?
- What is the other kind of food Jesus is talking about?
- Have you ever felt hungry for this other kind of food?
- Do you think Jesus means to suggest normal food is unimportant?
- In a way, the author of *The Family Story Bible* uses his imagination to fill in the blanks of what might have happened. Read this story from Luke 10:38–42. What did the author add? Can you imagine that Jesus *might* have done these extra things?

Exploring the story

There are many ways to explore this story. Below are some suggestions. Prepare at least two activities, so that people can choose the one that most interests them.

- **Drama:** Ask one person in your group to be Martha. Using the idea of a frozen tableau, move Martha's arms, legs, and body until she seems to express how Martha was. Is she smiling? Are her arms outstretched or on her hips? Does she look ready for action or rested? Would she look different at the beginning of the story than she did at the end?

- **Art:** If you are making a scrapbook of the superheroes of the Bible, add a picture of Martha.

- Sculpture: Make a clay model of one or more characters from this story.

- **Creative writing:** Write a mock diary entry for Martha. What do you think Martha would say about her day? What are her secrets, her inner thoughts?

- **Food:** Make a batch of hearty oatmeal muffins to feed a hungry traveller like Jesus. Cream together 1/2 cup (125 ml) sugar, 2 eggs, 1 cup (250 ml) sour cream. Add 1/2 teaspoon (2 ml) salt, 1 cup (250 ml) oatmeal, 1 cup (250 ml) flour, 1 teaspoon (5 ml) soda, 1/2 teaspoon (2 ml) baking powder. Put in greased muffin tins. Bake in 375°F (190°C) oven for 15–20 minutes. Makes one and a half dozen muffins.

- **Music:** Sing "Won't you come and sit with me," #78, *LifeSongs*.

- **Maps and patterns:** If you have access to the Internet, try searching for images of how various artists have seen Martha. How do the pictures differ? What may the artist be trying to express in each painting?

- **Serving others:** This is a wonderful opportunity to serve food to others. If you made the oatmeal muffins, with whom can you share them? If you did not make the muffins, make a commitment to serve food to someone in the near future.

Making the story part of your life

Ask people what they have learned from Martha today. Close with a circle prayer. Thank God for elements from Martha's story – hospitality, physical and spiritual food. Or have participants provide the name of a country in the world where food is needed, and ask God to watch over the people there.

Session 5
The boy who shares his meal

Session focus

A young boy shows that, when you share, there's lots to go around.

Gathering to hear the story

From your local newspaper, collect news items and pictures about children helping out in the community, such as through food drives and fundraising. Invite participants to look over the pictures and articles, and discuss why they think children are motivated to help in these ways.

Telling and talking about the story

Explain that the group will continue to look at superheroes of the Bible. Read the story "A child helps Jesus," from *The Family Story Bible,* p. 202. (Based on Matthew 14:13–21, Mark 6:31–44, Luke 9:10–17, John 6:1–13.)

To talk about the story, use questions like these:
- Do you have to be big and strong to be a hero?
- What are the character traits of this young hero?
- If you had been with Jesus, would you have had the nerve or vision to present a small gift of bread and fish? Talk about this.

Exploring the story

There are many ways to explore this story. Below are some suggestions. Prepare at least two activities, so that people can choose the one that most interests them.

- **Drama:** Do an object theatre play. Using kitchen objects as puppets, act out this story with your group. For instance, you may use toothpicks for the crowd, a large slotted spoon for Jesus, and a small teaspoon for the child. If possible, present your play to others.

- **Art:** If you are making a scrapbook, add a picture of the boy to your superhero album. Since this is the last session of this unit on superheroes, add a self-portrait with a caption like this: I can be a superhero of the faith. As you are drawing, talk about what kind of a superhero you would like to be.

- **Sculpture**: Use coloured pipe cleaners to create the figures in this story.

- **Creative writing:** Write a short paragraph from the point of view of a character in this story – the boy, Jesus, a disciple, or a member of crowd.

- **Music:** Sing "Feed us, Jesus," #104, *LifeSongs*.

- **Food:** Make a simple bread like bannock and heat up some fish sticks to eat with the bannock. Here is an easy recipe for bannock: Stir together 1/2 cup (125 ml) water, 4 tablespoons (60 ml) melted butter or bacon drippings, 4 tablespoons (60 ml) maple syrup or honey, 1/2 teaspoon (2 ml) salt (optional). Add 1 1/2 cups (375 ml) corn meal. Use 3 to 4 tablespoons (45–60 ml) cooking oil to fry the bannock. Turn the bread after five minutes.

- **Maps and patterns:** Lay out many different sheets of coloured construction paper. Decide which colours might stand for some of the characteristics of the people in the story. What colour is the tired Jesus? What colour is the cranky Philip? What colour is the laughing, scoffing Andrew? What colour is the generous boy?

- **Serving others:** Consider how you could share something in your fridge or pantry with others.

Making the story part of your life

Ask people what they have learned from the boy who helped Jesus. Talk about all the things the group has learned about superheroes of the Bible. Include all the ideas in a closing prayer.

Unit B
God's Crazy Timing

God's timing is often different from ours. This unit explores people from the Bible who discover God's crazy timing.

Hannah has a baby in
her old age
(*The Family Story Bible*, p. 105)

Elizabeth and Mary
become mothers
(*The Family Story Bible*, p. 158)

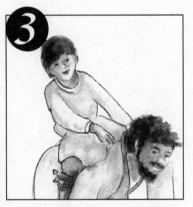

Jesus meets a child
(*The Family Story Bible*, p. 214)

Zacchaeus climbs a tree
(*The Family Story Bible*, p. 234)

A surprise on the road
to Emmaus
(*The Family Story Bible*, p. 260)

Session 1

Hannah has a baby in her old age

Session focus

Hannah is old, but she desperately wants a baby. In her old age, God hears her prayers, and she becomes a mother. Now that's crazy timing!

Gathering to hear the story

Before people gather, ask them to bring a baby picture of themselves. Look at the pictures and have participants take turns telling something they were told about themselves as a baby.

Telling and talking about the story

Explain that, together, you will be looking at God's crazy timing in the Bible. Today's story is about a much wanted child. Read the story "Hannah prays for a baby," from The Family Story Bible, p. 105. (Based on 1 Samuel 1 – 2.)

To talk about the story, use questions like these:
- What do you think Hannah thought of God's crazy timing – of giving her a baby in her old age?
- How do you think Hannah felt about leaving her beloved three-year-old at the temple with the old priest Eli?
- Have you ever had an experience where God's timing was different from your own?
- How did you deal with waiting for God? How did you feel about it at the end of your experience?

Exploring the story

There are many ways to explore this story. Below are some suggestions. Prepare at least two activities, so that people can choose the one that most interests them.

- **Drama:** If you have access to puppets, use the puppets to act out this story. If you have no puppets, use clean socks as hand puppets.

- **Art:** Make a cartoon strip that is four or five panels long. Participants may divide the story so that everyone draws one panel, or each person may make his or her own strip.

- **Sculpture:** Make a clay model of one or more characters from this story.

- **Creative writing:** Write a five-line cinquain (pronounced sin-cane) of thanks from Hannah's point of view. This is the pattern for a cinquain:

  Line 1 – one word (noun) title or name of the subject

  Line 2 – two words (adjectives) describing the subject

  Line 3 – three words (verbs) describing an action related to the subject

  Line 4 – four words describing a feeling about the subject, a complete sentence

  Line 5 – one word referring back to the subject of the poem

- **Music:** When Samuel is a little older, God gives him a message in the night. This is the first indication that Samuel will be a prophet for God. Sing a song that reflects what Samuel might have been thinking and feeling: "Here I am, Lord," #138, *LifeSongs*.

- **Food:** Make a "tabernacle meal" – dates, raisins, almonds, flat bread, milk.

God's Crazy Timing Unit B

- **Maps and patterns:** In a Bible atlas, find a picture of the interior of a tabernacle. The Bible says that Samuel was sleeping where the ark of God was. Look at the inside of the tabernacle and try to figure out where both Eli and Samuel might have been sleeping.

- **Serving others:** No doubt, Samuel made himself useful to Eli by running errands and doing small chores. With a partner, decide what small, helpful act you could do for someone this week.

Making the story part of your life

All of the stories in this unit are surprises that happen in homes and families. During this unit, end each session by repeating this family/home blessing, adapted from an old Irish blessing:

> God bless the corners of our lives
>
> And may our homes be blessed.
>
> And bless the stove, and bless the fridge,
>
> And bless each place of rest.
>
> And bless the rooftop overhead,
>
> And every sturdy wall.
>
> The joy of friends, the love of God,
>
> We pray for peace for all.

Session 2
Elizabeth and Mary
become mothers

> ### Session focus
>
> Two cousins – the older Elizabeth and the younger Mary – are both expecting babies at the same time. Both women come to believe that they will each have a special son. Now that's crazy timing!

Gathering to hear the story

Before people gather, ask participants to, if possible, bring a family portrait with a baby or young child in it. Invite them to talk about memories of when the youngest child arrived in the family. Was it long-awaited, sudden, shocking, chaotic? How did the adults respond? How did the children and youth respond? How did the grandparents respond?

Telling and talking about the story

Today's story looks at God's crazy timing in the story of Elizabeth and Mary. These women respond to the news that they will each soon have a baby. Read the story "Mary visits her cousin Elizabeth," from *The Family Story Bible*, p. 158. (Based on Luke 1:5–25, 39–80.)

To talk about the story, use questions like these:
- Elizabeth longed for a baby, but also must have felt strange when angels visited her, and then her husband couldn't speak. Describe how you think Elizabeth might have felt.
- How do you think Mary felt? Did she have mixed feelings?
- Why do you think that Zechariah was unable to speak while his wife Elizabeth was pregnant?
- What do you think Mary and Elizabeth talked about when they were together?

Exploring the story

There are many ways to explore this story. Below are some suggestions. Prepare at least two activities, so that people can choose the one that most interests them.

- **Drama:** Create a slide show or photo display. Act out scenes from this story and take pictures with a digital camera (for a slide show) or a disposable camera (for a photo display). Here is a list of shots to take:
  1. Portrait of Elizabeth and Zechariah.
  2. An angel talks to Elizabeth.
  3. Zechariah writes a note in a notebook for someone.
  4. Elizabeth greets or hugs Mary.
  5. Elizabeth pats her tummy, gives a strange look.
  6. Mary is singing.
  7. Mary and Elizabeth sip from teacups.
  8. Elizabeth and Zechariah wave goodbye to Mary.
  9. Elizabeth and Zechariah hold their baby, smiling.

- **Art:** Today's story occurs just before Christmas, so it is appropriate to do Christmas art. Make potato stamp wrapping paper. Cut a potato in half, lengthwise. Draw a Christmas symbol – star, bell, etc. – on the cut face of the potato. Using a paring knife, carefully outline the shape, cutting down into the potato. Then, from the side, cut away the edges so that the shape remains raised. Dip this raised symbol into poster paint and stamp it all over plain newsprint. After the paint has dried, save the paper for Christmas wrapping.

- **Sculpture:** Make sand-painted Christmas symbols. Mix builder's sand separately with various-coloured powdered tempera paints. Draw a Christmas symbol (star, manger, shepherd, etc.) on art paper. Paint the symbol with glue, then sprinkle on the sand with your finger tips to colour the symbol.

- **Creative writing:** Write a poem or song of thanks from Mary's or Elizabeth's point of view. Try writing the poem in gold or silver pen on black or dark blue paper, for the effect of God's light shining through a dark situation.

- **Music:** Sing together "'Twas in the moon of wintertime," #15, *LifeSongs*. This song conveys the sense of something unusual and hopeful happening in the middle of winter.

- **Food:** Make a graham wafer nativity stable, similar to how you would make a gingerbread house. Recipe for icing: In a large bowl, beat 3 egg whites until they begin to foam. Add 1 1/2 teaspoons (7 ml) cream of tartar and beat until the whites are stiff but not dry. Gradually beat in 3–3 1/2 cups (750–875 ml) icing sugar, beating for about five minutes until it reaches spreading consistency. Keep covered and refrigerated until needed. Use melted white chocolate as the glue and cover the graham wafers with the icing.

- **Maps and patterns:** Christians call the song that Mary sings "The Magnificat" (Mary's Song of Praise). From the Bible (Luke 1:46b–55) make a photocopy of this song for each member of the group. Pretend that you are ancient monks, wandering around the room reading the Magnificat aloud to yourselves. Non-readers in the group may hold hands with a reader and walk around with that person. Repeat the Magnificat so often in the coming week that you have it memorized.

- **Serving others:** Mary, Elizabeth and Zechariah were all excited about their babies soon to be born. Look around your community for people who are expecting babies. Is there some way you can help? Maybe by presenting baby gifts to a community prenatal class? Or by sending cards of encouragement to expectant mothers in your church?

Making the story part of your life

Ask what people have learned today about God's crazy timing. Close with this house/family blessing:

> God bless the corners of our lives
> And may our homes be blessed.
> And bless the stove, and bless the fridge,
> And bless each place of rest.
> And bless the rooftop overhead,
> And every sturdy wall.
> The joy of friends, the love of God,
> We pray for peace for all.

Session 3
Jesus meets a child

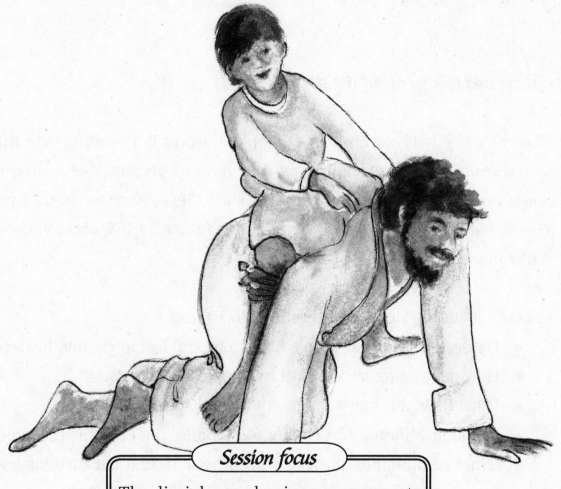

Session focus

The disciples are having an argument. In the middle of the argument, Jesus picks up a child to teach his disciples about living in God's new kingdom. Now that's crazy timing!

Gathering to hear the story

Find pictures of children from around the world. Look in magazines like *National Geographic* or on the Internet. Invite participants to discuss how the children in these photos are alike. How they are different from adults?

Telling and talking about the story

Today's story looks at another example of God's crazy timing. In this story, Jesus tells his disciples that they have to become like a child to enter the kingdom of heaven. Read the story "Jesus and the child," from *The Family Story Bible*, p. 214. (Based on Matthew 18:1–5, Mark 9:33–37, Luke 9:46–48.)

To talk about the story, use questions like these:

- Did Jesus mean that people have to be child*ish* to get into heaven?
- How does being childlike draw people closer to God?
- What does this story say to you about God's crazy timing?
- In Ralph Milton's *The Family Story Bible*, the child in this story is not running and playing with other children because his legs hurt and he gets sick if he runs too hard. This detail is not in any of the biblical versions of this same story. Why do you think that Ralph Milton added this detail?

Exploring the story

There are many ways to explore this story. Below are some suggestions. Prepare at least two activities, so that people can choose the one that most interests them.

- **Drama:** Act out this story with your group.
- **Art:** Using watercolour paints, draw a portrait of Jesus and a child surrounded by the disciples.
- **Sculpture:** Use the idea of "body sculpting" to describe how the individuals in this story might have felt. In body sculpting, a person makes a pose that communicates feeling, then freezes in that position until the others guess what emotion is being portrayed and who is being portrayed. For instance, the person who is body sculpting a disciple might pose with hands on hips and a frown on his or her face.
- **Creative writing:** Write an account of this encounter with Jesus from the child's point of view. Alternatively, research the word "shalom," which appears in this story.
- **Music:** Sing "Jesus' hands were kind hands," #124, *LifeSongs*.
- **Food:** Talk about food that children are able to prepare for themselves. Ask the children to serve something that is easy for them to get ready – crackers and cheese, fruit, ice cream, cookies.
- **Maps and patterns:** All three synoptic gospels record this story of Jesus and the child. Ask three different readers to each read one account (Matthew 18:1–5, Mark 9:33–37, Luke 9:46–48). How are they different? How are they the same? Each gospel

God's Crazy Timing Unit B

writer told the story from his own perspective, and that makes the stories all slightly different.

- **Serving others:** Jesus took time to play with a child. Talk about who you could invite to play with you this week. After school? A game of golf or tennis?

Making the story part of your life

Invite people to tell one thing they have learned about God's crazy timing from this story. Close with this house/family blessing:

God bless the corners of our lives

And may our homes be blessed.

And bless the stove, and bless the fridge,

And bless each place of rest.

And bless the rooftop overhead,

And every sturdy wall.

The joy of friends, the love of God,

We pray for peace for all.

Session 4
Zacchaeus climbs a tree

Session focus

Jesus talks to a short man –
who is sitting in a tree. Now
that's crazy timing!

Gathering to hear the story

Invite people to tell everything they know about the story of Zacchaeus. If they know a song about Zacchaeus, sing it together.

Telling and talking about the story

This story looks at another instance of God's crazy timing. Today you will look at how Jesus befriends Zacchaeus, a man who nobody liked. Read the story "Zacchaeus climbs a tree," from *The Family Story Bible*, p. 234. (Based on Luke 19:1–9.)

To talk about the story, use questions like these:
- Why did people dislike Zacchaeus?
- Why did Jesus single out Zacchaeus?
- When Jesus invited himself to Zacchaeus' house, people who would really disapprove of this action were all around him. Would you have been brave enough to invite yourself to an unpopular person's house if you were surrounded by friends who disapproved?
- What does this story say about God's crazy timing?

Exploring the story

There are many ways to explore this story. Below are some suggestions. Prepare at least two activities, so that people can choose the one that most interests them.

- **Drama:** Act out this story with your group. Make a tree by attaching green construction paper leaves to a chair.

- **Art:** Make life-size characters from this story. In a large room or hall, roll out long sheets of paper table cloth. Take turns lying on the paper while someone outlines your body with a pencil or marker. Cut out your body shape and dress it like someone in the story – Jesus, Zacchaeus, a Roman soldier, or a member of the crowd. Tape up these figures in your church hall or somewhere where people can enjoy the story.

- **Sculpture:** Make a diorama of a scene in the story, using salt dough – 2 cups (500 ml) plain flour, 1 cup (250 ml) table salt, 1 cup (250 ml) water. Provide twigs, straw, tissue paper and other small objects suitable for a Middle Eastern street. The scene may be made on sturdy boxboard and painted when dry.

- **Creative writing:** Write several "I am…" statements for both Jesus and Zacchaeus. For instance, Zacchaeus may say, "I am sorry," or "I am willing to repay the money I stole," and so on.

- **Music:** If your group knows the song "Zacchaeus was a wee little man," sing it together. Alternatively, sing "Jesus, you help," #122, *LifeSongs*.

- **Food:** It is quite possible that Zacchaeus climbed a fig sycamore. Buy and enjoy some fig bars, or make tea biscuits and add in some chopped figs.

- **Maps and patterns:** The story of Zacchaeus took place in Jericho. On a map of the Middle East in the time of Jesus, locate Jericho. Jesus and the disciples were on the way to Jerusalem. They would, of course, be walking. How far is it from Jericho to Jerusalem? How long do you estimate it would take to walk that distance?

- **Serving others:** In this story, Jesus invited himself to the home of someone who was unpopular. Make plans to follow Jesus' model, but in reverse. Decide if there is someone you know who has trouble making and keeping friends. Invite that person to your home for a meal.

Making the story part of your life

Talk about something you have learned about God's crazy timing from the Zacchaeus story. Close with this house/family blessing:

> God bless the corners of our lives
>
> And may our homes be blessed.
>
> And bless the stove, and bless the fridge,
>
> And bless each place of rest.
>
> And bless the rooftop overhead,
>
> And every sturdy wall.
>
> The joy of friends, the love of God,
>
> We pray for peace for all.

Session 5
A surprise on the road
to Emmaus

Session focus

Jesus' friends were *very* upset because he was dead. Then, suddenly, Jesus meets them on the road to Emmaus, but they don't recognize him. Now that's crazy timing!

Gathering to hear the story

Find pictures of famous people who have died and are fondly remembered, such as Elvis Presley, Johnny Cash, or Princess Diana. Invite participants to talk about what they remember most about the people pictured.

Telling and talking about the story

This is another story that explores God's crazy timing. In this story, Jesus appears to followers on the road to Emmaus, eats with them, and shatters conceptions of time by proving he is alive again. Read the story "On the road to Emmaus," from *The Family Story Bible*, p. 260. (Based on Luke 24:13–35.)

To talk about the story, use questions like these:
- What is the mood of Cleopas and Peter at the start of this story?
- Would you probably be sceptical (not able to believe) like them? Or, like Mary, would you be more convinced that Jesus was alive?
- Why do you think that Cleopas and Peter did not recognize Jesus?
- How would you feel on discovering, as they did at dinner, that Jesus was very much still with you?
- How does this story illustrate God's crazy timing?

Exploring the story

There are many ways to explore this story. Below are some suggestions. Prepare at least two activities, so that people can choose the one that most interests them.

- **Drama:** Play charades. Act out a character from this story and have the others guess who you are.

- **Art:** Make a diptych (two-panel artwork) in pastel or water colours. One panel should show the mood of Cleopas and Peter on the road, while the other panel shows their mood later at dinner. Mount the two pictures on joined panels of firm boxboard, such as a cereal box or small cardboard box.

- **Sculpture:** Take a small lump of play dough (see p. 60 for recipe) that can fit in the palm of your hand. Using thumbs only, create the face of someone in this story looking surprised, amazed, happy.

- **Creative writing:** Sometimes things are not what they seem. For some mysterious reason, Cleopas and Peter did not recognize Jesus. Write a mystery note about Jesus, using "invisible ink." With either lemon juice or milk, paint a message on paper with a paintbrush. Give the mystery note to someone in your group. When the note is dry, the recipient can press over it with a warm iron to make the message appear.

- **Music:** Sing "Jesus Christ is risen today," #57, or "Allelulia, alleluia, give thanks," #58, *LifeSongs*.

- **Food:** Make Irish soda bread to represent the bread Jesus broke with his friends in this story. Combine 2 cups (500 ml) flour, 1 cup (250 ml) whole-wheat flour, 1 tablespoon (15 ml) baking soda, 1 teaspoon (5 ml) baking powder, 1–2 cups (250–500 ml) buttermilk.

Mix well, to give a soft non-sticky dough. Do not knead. Mix only enough to bring the dough together. Form into a ball and flatten slightly onto a floured baking sheet. It is traditional to cut a cross on the top of the bread. Bake in a 375°F (190°C) oven for about 30–40 minutes, or until done. To check if the bread is done, turn the loaf over and tap the bottom. It should sound hollow.

- **Maps and patterns:** This story took place on a road to Emmaus. Using a map of the Middle East in the time of Jesus, locate Emmaus on the map. How far is it from Jerusalem, where Jesus was killed?

- **Serving others:** Make an extra loaf of the Irish soda bread (see recipe above) and take it to someone who is discouraged or sad.

Making the story part of your life

Since this is the last week in the unit "God's Crazy Timing," talk about all the things you have learned and enjoyed together. Close with this house/family blessing:

God bless the corners of our lives

And may our homes be blessed.

And bless the stove, and bless the fridge,

And bless each place of rest.

And bless the rooftop overhead,

And every sturdy wall.

The joy of friends, the love of God,

We pray for peace for all.

Unit C
Food for the Journey

The stories in this unit explore food for the journey. We share with our biblical friends the same need for and enjoyment of food. In these stories, food offers nurture, comfort, strength, and support. In addition, eating together creates community bonds. Once you've shared a meal with someone, you feel closer to them.

Special food on a journey
(*The Family Story Bible*, p. 86)

Martha learns about food
(*The Family Story Bible*, p. 223)

The Last Supper
(*The Family Story Bible*, p. 246)

Sharing
(*The Family Story Bible*, p. 271)

Dorcas and Anna
(*The Family Story Bible*, p. 276)

Session 1

Special food on a journey

Session focus

The people of God are hungry, thirsty, and grumbling on their long trip through the desert. Then, what a surprise! God provides a special food that tastes like "biscuits made with honey."

Gathering to hear the story

Set out different types of crackers and honey. As you smooth honey onto the crackers, ask participants if they remember a time when they were really hungry. Perhaps someone in your group, possibly an older person, remembers a time when there was not enough bread for the family and everyone went hungry.

Telling and talking about the story

Explain that you will be looking at food for the journey of life. Today's story is about special food that God provided for the Israelites in the desert. This bread, called manna, literally kept them alive. Read the story "Special food," from *The Family Story Bible*, p. 86. (Based on Exodus 16 – 17:7.)

To talk about the story, use questions like these:
- Why were the Israelites in the desert at the beginning of the story?
- What do you imagine a desert might be like?
- What does this story tell us about manna?
- When you find yourself upset, lonely, or hungry, do you remind yourself that God will provide, or do you grumble like the Israelites?

Exploring the story

There are many ways to explore this story. Below are some suggestions. Prepare at least two activities, so that people can choose the one that most interests them.

- **Drama:** Do an object theatre play. Using kitchen or cleaning utensils (brooms, mops) as puppets, act out this story with your group.

- **Art:** Make a manna-collecting basket. You will need balls of yarn, seven 30 cm pipe cleaners, ruler, scissors, and a round fruit such as a large orange or grapefruit. To make the basket, take three pipe cleaners in each hand and cross one bunch over the other. Tie them together in the middle with a long piece of yarn. Do not snip the yarn off. Separate the spokes to look like a wagon wheel. Wind the yarn over and under the spokes to form a 6 cm (2.5 inch) diameter base. Put the fruit on the base and bend the spokes up around it to shape the basket. Keeping the fruit in place, continue weaving to about 4 cm (1.5 inches) from the end of the spokes. Leaving two spokes up for a handle base, bend the rest of the spokes down. Trim the yarn, leaving a 5 cm (2 inch) tail. Tuck the tail under the nearest spoke. Twist the last pipe cleaner around the remaining ends for a handle. When you have finished creating the basket, set it on your kitchen or dining room table as a reminder of how God heard the cries of the hungry Israelites and sent manna to feed them.

- **Sculpture:** Use modelling clay to make baskets filled with manna.

- **Creative writing:** During this unit, create a newspaper that reports aspects of the stories. For instance, the items for this story might include a news report on the progress of the Israelites through the desert, a recipe for manna (crackers and honey), an ad for food or water, a birth announcement, etc. Use large sheets of paper, which can be added to as the unit proceeds.

- **Music:** Sing "To the banquet, come," #106, *LifeSongs*.

- **Food:** Make fry bread. Combine 3 cups (750 ml) flour, 1 tablespoon (15 ml) baking powder, 1/2 teaspoon (2 ml) salt. Add 1 cup (250 ml) warm water in small amounts, and knead dough until soft but not sticky. Adjust flour or water as needed. Cover bowl and let stand about 15 minutes. Pull off pieces of dough the size of eggs and roll out into thin rounds. Fry rounds in hot oil until bubbles appear on the dough. Turn over and fry on the other side until golden. Serve hot with honey brushed on top.

- **Maps and patterns:** Between two sturdy objects (you can use two chairs), string a length of twine. Using index cards, draw symbols that represent some aspect of this story. Today's symbols might be quails, bread, water. Hang the symbols on the twine with clothespins, and leave room to add other symbols from subsequent stories in this unit.

- **Serving others:** Talk about the current needs of your local food bank. Or, alternatively, talk with a social agency that helps people who struggle to provide enough food for their families. How might your group help?

Making the story part of your life

Together, light a Christ candle (a large, white candle with a cross carved in the side). Say, "This light reminds us that Jesus is like a light to the world." Ask people to discuss what they learned about food for the journey today. Talk about everyone's hopes, dreams, and worries for the day or week ahead. Pray together, then extinguish the flame.

Session 2

Martha learns about food

Session focus

Jesus shows Martha that there are two kinds of food.

Gathering to hear the story

Before your group gathers, form two displays. On one, put different kinds of food – bread, canned soup, fruit and vegetables. On the other, put objects like these: a classic book, a painting, a Bible, a musical instrument. As people gather, invite them to look over the two displays and try to guess what story the displays suggest.

Telling and talking about the story

Explain that you will be looking at food for the journey. This story about Jesus and Martha suggests that there are two types of food. Read the story "Martha learns about food," from *The Family Story Bible*, p. 223. (Based on Luke 10:38–42.)

To talk about the story, use questions like these:

- In your own words, describe the two types of food outlined in this story.
- Do you feel one kind of food is better than the other?
- Name some people who might need table food. Where can they get it?
- Name some people who might need spiritual food. Where can they get it?

Exploring the story

There are many ways to explore this story. Below are some suggestions. Prepare at least two activities, so that people can choose the one that most interests them.

- **Drama:** Make a story web as you retell the story. The person who starts the story holds a ball of yarn and tells the first part of the story. Holding on to the end of the yarn, that person tosses the ball of yarn to another person who tells another part. The second person holds on to the yarn and tosses the ball to someone else who tells more of the story. Continue until the story is complete and a web has been created.

- **Art:** In honour of Martha, make breadboards. Gather flat pieces of wood, sandpaper, paint, and brushes. Sand the board until it is smooth. Decorate it with paints. (If you are using enamel paint, be sure to wear a paint shirt.) Allow the board to dry for several days. As you work, listen to classical music.

- **Sculpture:** Make an edible sculpture. Prior to meeting, make bread dough and allow it to rise. After all hands are washed, divide the dough so everyone can create a bread sculpture (lying on its back). Cover with a clean tea towel. Allow to rise. Bake and enjoy.

- **Creative writing:** Continue work on the newspaper. Add a recipe page (physical food) and an arts page (food for the soul).

- **Music:** If someone in your group plays a musical instrument, invite him or her to play for you. Alternatively, play a CD of a favourite piece of music that lifts the spirits.

- **Food:** Make Martha's stick-to-your-ribs oatmeal banana muffins. Cream 1/2 cup (125 ml) white sugar and 1/2 cup (125 ml) margarine. Beat in 2 eggs, 3 mashed, over-ripe bananas, and 3/4 cup (180 ml) honey. Stir together 1 1/2 cups (375 ml) flour, 1 teaspoon (5 ml) baking powder, 1 teaspoon (5 ml) baking soda, and 3/4 teaspoon (3 ml) salt. Add to the creamed mixture, beating only until just blended. Stir in 1 cup (250 ml) quick oatmeal. Fill 24 medium muffin cups about two thirds full. Bake at 375°F (190°C) for 15–17 minutes.

- **Maps and patterns:** If you have a Bible dictionary, research the type of food that would have been commonly eaten in Jesus' time. For many people in Jesus' time, the hunger for the "other kind of food" would have been satisfied by studying the Torah. Using the Bible dictionary, find out something about the Torah.

- **Serving others:** If you have a specific skill – drawing, making crafts, playing a musical instrument – talk together about where you could share this with others. Nursing and retirement homes or community clubs for children may be a good place to look.

Making the story part of your life

Together, light a Christ candle. Say, "This light reminds us that Jesus is like a light to the world." Ask people to discuss what they have learned about food for the journey today. Talk about everyone's hopes, dreams, and worries for the day or week ahead. Pray together, then extinguish the flame.

Session 3

The Last Supper

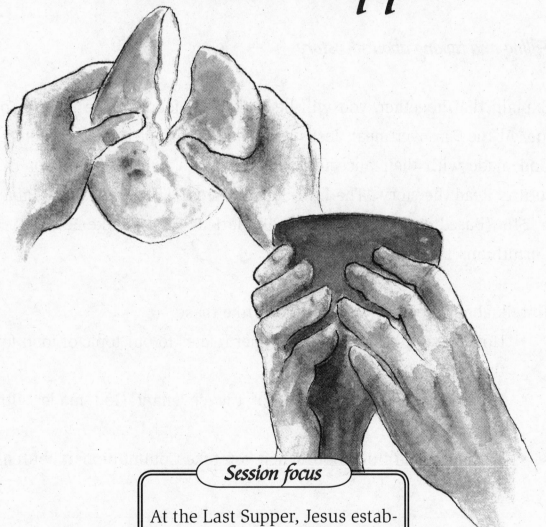

Session focus

At the Last Supper, Jesus establishes a simple mealtime ritual that reminds us that God is with us always.

Gathering to hear the story

Before people gather, find a chalice and plate used for Communion. As people gather, invite them to talk about their memories of Communion – their first Communion, their most memorable one, and so on.

Telling and talking about the story

Explain that, together, you will be looking at food for the journey of life. At the Passover meal, Jesus reminds the disciples of the covenant God made with their ancestors, and creates a new covenant for the future. Read the story "The Last Supper," from *The Family Story Bible*, p. 246. (Based on Matthew 26:26–29, Mark 14:22–25, Luke 22:17–20, 1 Corinthians 11:23–26.)

To talk about the story, use questions like these:

- How do you think the Last Supper relates to our topic of food for the journey?
- What are some other signs of the covenant God made with humanity?
- What do you think about when you take Communion at church?

Exploring the story

There are many ways to explore this story. Below are some suggestions. Prepare at least two activities, so that people can choose the one that most interests them.

- **Drama:** Find a picture of Leonardo da Vinci's painting of the Last Supper. (This is easily found on the Internet by typing "da Vinci Last Supper" into a search engine, such as Google.) Dress in biblical costume for a photo, then strike the same pose as the disciples in the painting. (Although the disciples were male, it is perfectly fine to have male and female disciples in your picture.) When the picture is done, display it in a prominent place with the caption, "Disciples of Jesus."

- **Art:** As a group, try to replicate the Last Supper painting by Leonardo da Vinci. You will need a long piece of mural paper, paints, and brushes for everyone in the group.

- **Sculpture:** Using self-hardening clay, shape a chalice and plate for Communion. After they are dry, paint them with a glaze.

- **Creative writing:** If you are creating a newspaper, add a page for "breaking news," with accounts of Jesus breaking bread at the Last Supper. Add a piece of intrigue about possible treason in the ranks (Judas). Alternatively, write a litany that can be used at a Communion service. The litany can express needs for the world with the response line being, "I'm giving you God's promise again." Here is an example:

    Leader: Oh God, our people are hungry in Malawi.

    People: I'm giving you God's promise again.

Leader: Oh God, bombing in the Middle East continues.

People: I'm giving you God's promise again.

- **Music:** Sing "To the banquet, come," #106, *LifeSongs*.

- **Food:** Make unleavened bread for Communion. Here is a simple recipe: Combine 3 cups (750 ml) flour and 1 teaspoon (5 ml) salt. In a separate bowl, beat together 3 eggs and 2 tablespoons (30 ml) oil. Add egg mixture to flour, then add 1/2 cup (125 ml) water or milk. Beat for two to three minutes. Pour into three eight-inch square pans, greased, and bake for 20 minutes in a 450°F (230°C) oven.

- **Maps and patterns:** Lay out on a table all the various pictures you can find of people celebrating Communion – both in the Last Supper and contemporary pictures. (See if your church has any picture files of Communion.) What do you notice about these representations?

- **Serving others:** As a group or family, offer to bake bread or prepare the bread and wine for the next Communion service at your church.

Making the story part of your life

Together, light a Christ candle. Say, "This light reminds us that Jesus is like a light to the world." Ask people to discuss what they have learned about food for the journey today. Talk about everyone's hopes, dreams, and worries for the day or week ahead. Pray together, then extinguish the flame.

Session 4

Sharing

Session focus

The early Christians loved to eat together, sharing food for the journey.

Gathering to hear the story

Before people gather, find newspaper articles or pictures of your local food bank. As people are gathering, share what you know about your food bank – location, families served, time of year of major drives, and so on.

Telling and talking about the story

Explain that, together, your group will continue to explore the importance of eating together in Christian community. Today's story looks at ways the early followers of Jesus continued to share meals after his death and resurrection. Read the story "Sharing," from *The Family Story Bible*, p. 271. (Based on Acts 4:32 – 5:11.)

To talk about the story, use questions like these:
- Talk about a time when someone you love (such as a parent or grandparent) came to visit, and you felt sad when they left. How did you remember them?
- What did the early Christians remember about Jesus?
- If you had to explain "the Christ" to a friend, what would you say?
- Why is it so difficult for people to learn to share?

Exploring the story

There are many ways to explore this story. Below are some suggestions. Prepare at least two activities, so that people can choose the one that most interests them.

- **Drama:** Use pantomime (actions but no words) to act out things that the early Christians might have shared together. Cut up slips of paper with an individual word on each – food, money, clothes, toys, recipes, water, wine, oil. Taking turns, pick one word and pantomime it until the others guess what was shared.

- **Art:** Make a graffiti wall by posting large sheets of paper in an open area. Add the title "Sharing is…" and, as a group, write or draw as many ideas and experiences of sharing as you can think of.

- **Sculpture:** Prior to this session, invite everyone in the group to bring a box of food – cereal, macaroni and cheese, pancake mix, etc. – to donate to the food bank. Make a food pyramid using the boxes. Or you can make a tin can pyramid. Leave your food sculpture as a display in your congregation, so that others will be reminded of the need to share food in your community.

- **Creative writing:** Have each participant write a short monologue from the point of view of one of the early Christians – a woman, a man, a youth, a child. In pairs, read your monologues to each other, both reading at the same time. You will find that it is hard to have a "dialogue" when no one is listening. Read your monologues to each other a second time, but, this time, take turns and listen carefully to the reader.

- **Music:** Sing "We are the church," #133, *LifeSongs*.

- **Food:** Make sour cream cornbread to share with others. Mix together 3/4 cup (180 ml) yellow corn meal, 1 cup (250 ml) flour, 1/4 cup (60 ml) sugar, 2 teaspoons (10 ml) baking powder, 1/2 teaspoon (2 ml) baking soda, 3/4 teaspoon (3 ml) salt. In a second bowl, combine 1 cup (250 ml) sour cream, 1/4 cup (60 ml) milk, 1 egg (beaten), 2 tablespoons (30 ml) oil. Mix all ingredients just enough to blend well. Pour into a greased eight-inch square pan. Bake at 425°F (220°C) for about 20–25 minutes. Serves six to eight people.

- **Maps and patterns:** Use the concept of mind mapping to show the effects of sharing. You will need a large sheet of paper and some markers. Draw a circle and, in it, write an act of sharing, such as, "I gave away my extra pen in class," or "I had two apples in my lunch so I gave one to a friend." Think about how a simple act of sharing might affect the person to whom you gave something. Draw a line or "thread" to a second circle and in that circle write an idea of how *that* person might have shared with someone else. Keep going until the entire sheet is filled, with each act of sharing inspiring another one. The group will see that sharing has a domino effect.

- **Serving others:** As a group or individuals, volunteer at your local food bank.

Making the story part of your life

Together, light a Christ candle. Say, "This light reminds us that Jesus is like a light to the world." Ask people to discuss what they have learned about food for the journey today. Talk about everyone's hopes, dreams, and worries for the day or week ahead. Pray together, then extinguish the flame.

Session 5

Dorcas and Anna

Session focus

Dorcas' love for Christ shows in her many acts of kindness – sewing and giving food to others.

Gathering to hear the story

Before people gather, create a display about outreach projects your church or family takes on. As people gather, talk about these projects.

Telling and talking about the story

Explain that, together, you will hear the story of one of the most gracious and beloved women in the early church. Dorcas was a very practical saint! Read the story "Dorcas and Anna help each other," from *The Family Story Bible*, p. 276. (Based on Acts 9:36–42.) The author of *The Family Story Bible* writes at the top of this story that he uses his imagination to create a story of how Dorcas might have helped a young homeless girl, Anna. Take time to read the biblical account of this story as well.

To talk about the story, use questions like these:
- If you met Dorcas in person, what do you think she would be like?
- How do you think Peter succeeds in waking Dorcas?
- Dorcas was both experienced and talented in sewing and cooking. Do you have to be good at these things to help provide food for others?
- What gave Dorcas the drive and energy to keep working to help others?

Exploring the story

There are many ways to explore this story. Below are some suggestions. Prepare at least two activities, so that people can choose the one that most interests them.

- **Drama:** Act out this story with your group and, if possible, present your play to another group.

- **Art:** Make a sharing chain. On strips of coloured paper, write in large letters ideas of how each person can share things with others. Loop the strips and attach them together in a chain with the ideas on the outside of the paper strips. Hang the sharing chain over a bulletin board in your church that tells of a sharing or outreach project your church does.

- **Sculpture:** Make papier mâché bread bowls which can be used by your congregation for shared meals or by your family. To make papier mâché, you will need newspaper and a large bowl of flour paste (flour mixed with water). Dip strips of newspaper into the flour paste and shape over an inflated balloon until it looks like a bowl. Set aside to dry completely (two or three days). When it is dry, paint the bowl in a bright colour using acrylic paint. (Wear a paint smock.)

- **Creative writing:** Write a diary entry from Anna's point of view about her encounter with Dorcas.

- **Music:** Sing "Jesus, you help," #122, *LifeSongs*.

- **Food:** Dorcas probably wanted to not only help Anna fill her stomach, but also give her a nutritious meal. Make a nutritious pizza with your group. Top the pizza with meat, cheese, tomato sauce, and chopped vegetables such as onion and green pepper.

- **Maps and patterns:** Get a piece of paper and some pencil crayons. On the left side of the paper write the names of everyone in your group or family. On the opposite side write an idea of how you might share something with that person in the week ahead.

- **Serving others:** As a group, gather together contents of a kit to be distributed by the Mennonite Central Committee. This group distributes kits for AIDS, health, newborn, relief, school, and sewing. See www.mcc.org and look under "donate," then under "kits and material resources." Alternatively, if you sew, this is a good opportunity to make something warm, such as a simple blanket from a piece of fleece. This can be donated to a child who must stay temporarily at a women's shelter.

Making the story part of your life

Together, light a Christ candle. Say, "This light reminds us that Jesus is like a light to the world." Ask people to discuss what they have learned about food for the journey today, and throughout the unit. Talk about everyone's hopes, dreams, and worries for the day or week ahead. Pray together, then extinguish the flame.

Unit D
Bully for You!

This unit explores bullying. There were bullies in the Bible and, sadly, there are still bullies in society today. This unit helps participants think about bullying, and inspires us to keep working on this difficult issue. These stories are used:

Samson and Delilah
(*The Family Story Bible*, p. 100)

David and Goliath
(*The Family Story Bible*, p. 109)

A mean trick on Jesus
(*The Family Story Bible*, p. 218)

Saul learns about Jesus
(*The Family Story Bible*, p. 274)

You are God's temple
(1 Corinthians 3:10–17.
This story doesn't appear in
The Family Story Bible)

Session 1

Samson and Delilah

Session focus

The Bible has stories of bullies in action. The story about Samson is one of them. We can learn from reflecting and acting on this story.

Gathering to hear the story

Before you begin this unit, take time to think through some of the issues that may arise. Has someone in your group been bullied? Has someone acted like a bully? Does someone have painful memories of a loved one being treated badly?

Before people gather, find scenes or settings in magazine pictures that show where bullying can happen – school, workplace, church. As people of different ages gather, talk about the pictures and the kinds of bullying that might go on in each place.

Telling and talking about the story

Explain that your group will examine Bible stories that say something about bullying and how we can help to overcome it. Before reading this session's story, remind people that, in addition to bullying, this is a Bible story with a lot of violence and killing. Ask listeners to keep this question in their minds: Who is the bully in the story? Read the story "Samson and Delilah," from *The Family Story Bible*, p. 100. (Based on Judges 16.)

To talk about the story, use questions like these:
- Just who exactly are the bullies in this story?
- Samson still calls on God for help, even in one of his darkest moments. What does that say about Samson's faith? About the source of his strength?

- The story says that Samson was hated, not so much because he was strong, but because he used his strength to kill a lot of Philistines. What do you think about the suggestion that, if you believe in God and stay close to God, it is acceptable to kill other people?
- Do you think you would have the faith to pray for God's help if you were being bullied?

Exploring the story

There are many ways to explore this story. Below are some suggestions. Prepare at least two activities, so that people can choose the one that most interests them.

- **Drama:** There is a lot of talk about killing in the story of Samson. Use body sculpting (putting your body in a "frozen" position) to describe how you think God felt about all this killing.
- **Art:** Using photos and articles from magazines and newspapers, make a collage on a sheet of poster board. Add a title like, "Bullying *must* stop," or "This is a no bullying zone," or "This is a respect zone."
- **Sculpture:** Divide into groups of three and do frozen tableaus of three people – a bully, a bullied person, and a bystander. Show your tableau to others.
- **Creative writing:** Write a prayer of confession on teardrop shapes. Use the prayer with your group.
- **Music:** Sing "Jesus, you help," #122, or "Forgive our sins as we forgive," #125, *LifeSongs*.

- **Food:** Prepare and share foods that make us strong – protein foods (meat, nuts, cheese, eggs) and fruit and vegetables. As you eat, talk about the challenge Christians have to use their strength to express God's love and goodness.

- **Maps and patterns:** Invite a teacher to come as a guest. Ask your guest to describe patterns that he or she has seen on schoolyards or in classrooms that would be classified as bullying. Ask what strategies have been helpful to stop bullying behaviour in these situations. Alternatively, youth and adults who can purchase Barbara Coloroso's book *The Bully, the Bullied, and the Bystander*[1] can make a commitment to read the book and give a book report at a subsequent meeting.

- **Serving others:** In her book, Barbara Coloroso makes a distinction between *tattling* and *telling*. Children should not tattle on each other, but if children are being hurt or bullied, they should tell an adult so the adult can help. Help children make this distinction by creating a chart entitled, "The difference between tattling and telling." Add this information:

Tattling: If it will only get another child *in* trouble, don't tell me.

Telling: If it will get you or another child *out* of trouble, tell me.

[1] Barbara Coloroso, *The Bully, the Bullied, and the Bystander* (Harper Collins, 2002).

Making the story part of your life

Ask people to discuss what they have learned today about bullying. Use a guided meditation to close this session. Invite people to sit comfortably with their hands in their laps and eyes closed. Read slowly and quietly:

> There are dark storm clouds in your day. The wind is strong and pushes you in ways that you do not want to go. But wait…step through here.
>
> Step through a gateway into God's garden. Your friends are in the garden, waiting for you, smiling and happy. There are beautiful flowers and grass-green trees. A stream murmurs as it passes over rocks. Everything is calm and peaceful. There are animals in the garden, too – a lion and a lamb. But they do not bother each other and they do not bother you. Everything is quiet and calm. You are in a world that God has created. It is full of warm sunshine and the air is clear. A soft breeze makes the leaves rustle over your head. You know that you are close to God. Everything is calm, peaceful, and still. This is the day that the Lord has made. Let us rejoice and be glad in it. Amen.

Session 2

David and Goliath

Session focus

David faces and defeats a big bully. He knows God is with him.

Gathering to hear the story

Before people arrive, find pictures of cartoon, movie, or comic book bullies, such as Binkie Barns from Arthur, Flats the flatfish from SpongeBob SquarePants, the Joker from Batman, Voldemort from Harry Potter, Darth Vader from Star Wars. As people gather, identify the bullies and talk about the traits of bullies. (See Maps and patterns in this session for a list of characteristics.)

Telling and talking about the story

Explain that the group will continue to think about bullying. The story for this session is about a huge bully – Goliath. Read the story, "David and Goliath," from *The Family Story Bible*, p. 109. (Based on 1 Samuel 17, with portions from chapters 16, 18 and 19.)

To talk about the story, use questions like these:
- What was David's main weapon for defeating Goliath?
- Do you have to be a big person to stop a bully?
- Have you ever been bullied?
- How did you get out of this bullying situation?
- Do you think it was right for David to kill the bully?

Exploring the story

There are many ways to explore this story. Below are some suggestions. Prepare at least two activities, so that people can choose the one that most interests them.

- **Drama:** Do role plays based on one or both of these scenarios:

  1. Andrew was born with a speech impediment. Although he is a good student, he is consistently teased about his speech by one of his classmates. His classmate and two or three other boys begin to follow Andrew home from school. They never actually touch or hurt Andrew, but they imitate his speech patterns. You are following this group of boys and are troubled by their behaviour. You decide to confide in your teacher. Role play the conversation between you and your teacher.

  2. You have known Sarah for 10 years, since you started school together. Lately, she has been acting very strange, often ignoring you and hanging out with more popular girls. Yesterday you found out that Sarah has been gossiping about you in a chat room on the Internet. This upsets you and you decide to talk this over with your Dad. Role play this conversation.

- **Art:** Make a comic strip. Fold legal size paper in quarters or eighths and draw the story of David and Goliath. Use word balloons to express the bullying component. Can you put this cartoon in your church newsletter?

- **Sculpture:** Use modelling clay to create something that expresses your reaction to this story.
- **Creative writing:** Create a prayer journal. This can continue throughout the unit. Here are suggestions for page titles, if desired:
  - When I am frightened
  - When I've noticed God in my life
  - When I've noticed God in nature
  - Times when I tried to help someone
  - Things I try not to do
- **Music:** Sing "God be with you," #112, *LifeSongs*.
- **Food:** In the story, David's father sends him to the field with some food for his brothers. Talk about what David might have packed – a stew? fruit or nuts? bread? Pack a lunch like David did; take a short trip (to another room); enjoy your picnic with David's brothers. To increase the drama, dress for dinner by wearing biblical style clothes.
- **Maps and patterns:** Make a list of the characteristics of bullies. Here are some, as outlined by Barbara Coloroso:[2]
  - like to dominate other people
  - like to use other people to get what they want
  - find it hard to see a situation from the other person's point of view
  - are concerned only with their own wants and pleasures, not the needs, rights, and feelings of others
  - tend to hurt others when parents or other adults are not around
  - view weaker siblings or peers as prey

[2] Ibid., 20.

- use blame, criticism, and false allegations to project their own inadequacies onto their target
- refuse to accept responsibility for their actions
- lack foresight
- crave attention

- **Serving others:** Buy a copy of *The Bully, the Bullied, and the Bystander,* by Barbara Coloroso (Harper Collins, 2002). With your group, flip through the book, reading some of the chapter titles. Decide where you might donate this book – a school library, your church library, a youth drop-in centre.

Making the story part of your life

Ask people to discuss what they have learned today about bullying. Use a guided meditation to close this session. Invite people to sit comfortably with their hands in their laps and eyes closed. Read slowly and quietly:

It is a cold and windy day. Everything is grey...grey...grey. But wait...step through here.

Step through a gateway into God's colour garden. It is a garden shimmering in light. Over here is deep purple periwinkle nestled in a bed of shining greenery. Over there are primroses in every shade of the rainbow – yellow, violet, blue, red. There are peach-leafed bellflowers and dusty millers with their lamb's ear leaves and soft pink flowers. Everything is calm, peaceful and still... Gone are all the cold greys. Welcome the vibrant colours in the Creator's paint box. This is the day that the Lord has made. Let us rejoice and be glad in it. Amen.

Session 3

A mean trick on Jesus

Session focus

Some bullies try to trick Jesus, but he has a wise answer that shows God's love.

Gathering to hear the story

Before people gather, find a picture of Rosa Parks on the bus. (Use a search engine to find photos on the Internet, or find a library book on the civil rights movement.)

As people gather, determine and discuss who is in the picture. What is she famous for?

Telling and talking about the story

Explain that, together, your group will examine another Bible story that depicts bullying. This story looks at how Jesus outwitted some bullies who were trying to trick him into saying something against the law. Read the story "A mean trick on Jesus," from *The Family Story Bible*, p. 218. (Based on John 8:1–11.)

To talk about the story, invite people to break into small intergenerational groups, and use questions like these:

- Who is the real "bad guy" in this story?
- Does Jesus have to do anything violent, like throw stones, to defeat these bullies?
- Is it possible to defeat bullies today through peaceful methods?
- Describe how the woman must have felt at the end of this story.
- Do you think you would have had the courage of Rosa Parks or Jesus?

Exploring the story

There are many ways to explore this story. Below are some suggestions. Prepare at least two activities, so that people can choose the one that most interests them.

- **Drama:** Look at the pictures of the three men from *The Family Story Bible*, p. 218. Describe what each might be thinking.

- **Art:** In the story, the Pharisees walk away, and the woman is instructed by Jesus to go away too, but to try to grow in God's way. Make sand footprints, and when they are dry, put them on a bulletin board with the caption, "Walk in God's way." To make the footprints, trace your foot on a piece of construction paper. Cut out the footprint and tape it to a larger piece of construction paper. Using a brush, spread white glue around the edge of the footprint. Sprinkle sand on the glue and remove the top footprint.

- **Sculpture:** Make an inukshuk. This human shaped Inuit landscape marker is an excellent image for reminding us that humanity is at the heart of even the most forbidding landscape. Search for images of an inukshuk on the Internet or in the library. Make your inukshuk from small stones, or use air-drying clay.

- **Creative writing:** If you began a prayer journal last week, continue to write in it. Alternatively, write a thank you note to Jesus from the woman he saved.

- **Music:** Sing "God gave me a life to live," #98, or "I am thanking Jesus," #101, *LifeSongs*.

- **Food:** Enjoy a simple snack of fruit and cheese.

- **Maps and patterns:** Using a Bible dictionary, find out what you can about the Pharisees. Who were they? Why were they trying to trick Jesus?

- **Serving others:** Explore community groups who work with restorative justice. Alternatively, download stories from the Centre for Restorative Justice website (www.sfu.ca/crj).

Making the story part of your life

Ask people to discuss what they have learned today about bullying. Ask group members what they would like included in a prayer, then close with prayer.

Session 4

Saul learns about Jesus

Session focus

A bully joins the People of the Way.

Gathering to hear the story

Before people gather, find one or two pictures of Scrooge from Charles Dickens' *A Christmas Carol*. As people gather, form pairs of different ages to talk about what makes Scrooge a bully at the beginning of the story. Does he change? What causes him to change?

Telling and talking about the story

Explain that, together, the group will hear a Bible story about someone who started out as an intense bully, but ended up as a fervent disciple of Jesus. Read the story "Saul learns about Jesus," from *The Family Story Bible*, p. 274. (Based on Acts 9:1–19, 22:3–16, 26:4–18.)

To talk about the story, invite people to break into small intergenerational groups, and use questions like these:

- What do we know about Saul when this story begins?
- What changed him?
- Have you ever bullied anyone?
- Have you ever had a similar experience, one that dramatically changed your worldview and behaviour – for the better?

Exploring the story

There are many ways to explore this story. Below are some suggestions. Prepare at least two activities, so that people can choose the one that most interests them.

- **Drama:** Role play one or both of these scenarios:

1. You have a younger brother and it seems to you that your parents favour him and let him get away with doing things that you can't do. Sometimes you are so angry at him that you want to really hurt him. One day, when the two of you are alone, you pinch him very hard, and he screams in pain. This incident scares you and you decide to tell your older sister. Role play this conversation.

2. When you were a child, your parents spanked you when you did something naughty. You don't like the idea of hitting a child for being naughty, but sometimes you find yourself swatting your child when he is too unruly. You are upset with yourself and decide to talk this over with your spouse. Role play this conversation.

- **Art:** Create a white on black chalk drawing. Depict the story of Saul in three or four scenes, using white art chalk on black paper. The drawing will highlight the element of light in the darkness in this story.
- **Sculpture:** Using modelling clay, form the picture of Saul that the artist has depicted in *The Family Story Bible*, on page 274.

- **Creative writing:** If you are writing a prayer journal, add more to it. Alternatively, write a letter from Saul/Paul to his family back home, telling them what happened.
- **Music:** Sing "What does it mean to follow Jesus?" #165, *LifeSongs*.
- **Food:** In the story, Saul had not eaten for many days, because he was blind and could not help himself. When Ananias came to visit and restored Saul's sight, Paul told Ananias that he was very hungry. What do you think Ananias gave him to eat? Perhaps bread, cheese, and beans? Enjoy an Ananias feast of bread, cheese, and beans.
- **Maps and patterns:** Saul was blind in two ways. He was physically blind for a few days, and he was spiritually blind because he could not accept Jesus. Make two columns entitled "physically blind" and "spiritually blind." How can you help people who are physically blind? How can you help people who are spiritually blind?
- **Serving others:** When Saul's name was changed to Paul, he became incredibly active in travelling and telling others that Jesus was the Christ, that Jesus was resurrected from the dead, and that Jesus had died to make things right between God and humanity. Talk about ways you can share with others the good news of what Jesus has done. Could you give away Bible story books in your community? Could you invite someone to church?

Making the story part of your life

Ask, "What is one thing you have learned about bullying?" Invite people to share, but it is not necessary that everyone say something aloud.

Close with a circle prayer. Everyone holds hands, and the leader invites the group to thank God for elements from Saul's story – God's love is for all, God's love can cause bullies to turn around. If someone does not wish to pray aloud, he or she simply squeezes the hand of the next person, and that person continues.

Session 5

You are God's temple

Session focus

You are God's temple. Together with God, you are building a strong and wholesome life.

Gathering to hear the story

Before people gather, collect some building blocks, such as Lego. As people arrive, invite them to build something, making sure that the foundation is particularly strong.

Telling and talking about the story

Explain that, together, your group will end the unit on bullying by looking at a letter written to the early Christians from a former bully – the apostle Paul. This letter is not included in *The Family Story Bible*, but it can be read from the Bible. Read 1 Corinthians 3:10–17.

To talk about the scripture, invite people to break into small intergenerational groups, and use questions like these:

- What are your thoughts when you consider that these lines were written by a man who once persecuted Christians?
- Are there times when you find it difficult to believe that you are God's temple?
- Have you ever had an experience that makes it hard for you to act as if everyone is holy?
- What can you do to help yourself remember and go through life fully convinced that these statements are true?

Exploring the story

There are many ways to explore this story. Below are some suggestions. Prepare at least two activities, so that people can choose the one that most interests them.

- **Drama:** If you were going to present the scripture from this session (1 Corinthians 3:10–17) in visual form for your congregation, how would you do that? Brainstorm ideas. Inquire as to whether your group can make a presentation on bullying to your congregation. Using a visual presentation, convey the ideal that God has for us – we are to build our lives until we become a holy temple.

- **Art:** Use pictures from newspapers and magazines to create a large collage that illustrates the idea, "You are God's temple."

- **Sculpture:** Using the building blocks (Lego), build a structure that does not have a solid foundation. What happens to these structures? Talk about how to change this. Have you met anyone who seems like this – without a solid foundation in life?

- **Creative writing:** Add more to your prayer journal.

- **Music:** Sing "What does it mean to follow Jesus?" #165, or "The Great Commandments," #172, LifeSongs.

- **Food:** Prepare and serve food that builds strong bones – milk products, salmon. Talk about what happens if people cannot or are unwilling to eat foods that help develop strong bones. If you have a chart of food guides for healthy living, share it with the group.

- **Maps and patterns:** If you have small children in your group, some may not know what a temple is. Using a Bible dictionary, find a picture of the temple that Solomon built. It was a massive building. Talk about the need for a strong foundation.

- **Serving others:** Talk about what you can do to communicate what you have learned about bullying to others in your church or community.

Making the story part of your life

Take a few minutes and list all the things you have learned about bullying.

Close with prayer. Invite the group to thank God for the idea from Paul's letter that everyone is God's temple, worthy of compassionate treatment. God's love is for all. Or contribute the name of a person, type of person, or group that needs God's particular protection or a reminder of God's love.

Annotated Bibliography of All-Ages Resources

General

Across the Generations: Incorporating All Ages in Ministry: The Why and How. Augsburg Fortress, 2001. Learn how to minister across generations with this resource and companion CD.

Aleshire, Daniel O. *Faith Care: Ministering To All God's People Through The Ages Of Life.* Westminster Press, 1988. The author illustrates how paying attention to people of all ages can be the basis for ministry, education, and Christian nurture.

Carroll, Jackson W., and Wade Clark Roof. *Bridging Divided Worlds: Generational Cultures in Congregations.* Jossey-Bass, 2002. With an abundance of information and commentary, this book shows how congregations are learning ways to bridge the gaps and connect the various worlds the generations inhabit, to create stronger, richer, and more vibrant religious communities.

Lewis, Diane. *Generation Mixing.* www.elca.org/lp/generati.html. An online article about intentional intergenerational learning.

Linking the Generations, an issue of the *APCE Advocate*, Spring 2006, Volume 31, Number 1. A series of articles on linking the generations in local congregations.

Loper, Edward A. *Building an Intergenerational Church*. Louisville: Geneva Press, 1999. This short, easy-to-read booklet describes the changing intergenerational landscape and suggests models for intergenerational ministry.

McIntosh, Gary L. *One Church, Four Generations: Understanding and Reaching All Ages in Your Church*. Baker Books, 2002. This book provides insight into the four generations found in churches.

No More Us & Them: 100 Ways to Bring Your Youth & Church Together. Group Publishing, 1999. This immensely practical book contains idea after idea for making bonds and links between generations.

Rendle, Gilbert R. *The Multigenerational Congregation: Meeting the Leadership Challenge*. Alban Institute, 2002. To successfully serve many persons in the 21st century, multigenerational congregations must 1. understand their situations and assumptions and 2. develop new skills to capitalize on their potential for health.

Westerhoff, John H. lll, and Gwen Kennedy Neville. *Generation to Generation*. Pilgrim Press, 1974. Although an older book, this book was surely ahead of its time! It focuses on how religion and culture are transmitted from adults to child in religious-cultural communities.

White, James W. *Intergenerational Religious Education*. Religious Education Press, 1988. A scholarly examination of models of intergenerational religious education, relevant theories, curriculum, and evaluation strategies.

Whitesel, Bob and Kent R. Hunter. *A House Divided: Bridging the Generation Gaps in Your Church*. Abingdon Press, 2001. This book provides seven steps to move any church from a one-generational bias to a healthy tri-generational balance.

Wilk, Karen, ed. *Together All God's People: Integrating Children and Youth into the Life of Your Church*. Faith Alive Christian Resources, 2005. Implement these strategies, resources, and action plans to make your church a multigenerational community.

Learning Together

Celebrating God's Hospitality: Four Intergenerational Meals on Creation, World Hunger and Justice. www.elca.org/hunger/resources/ Hospitality.

Finley, Kathy, et al. *Growing Together: Six Intergenerational Celebrations.* Morehouse Publishing/Living the Good News, 1999, 2001. These books explore the meaning of key celebrations through group discussions, stories, games, art, and community activities. Volume one includes celebrations for Building a Parish Family, All Saints' Day, Thanksgiving, Advent, Christmas, and Epiphany. Volume two contains sessions for Mardi Gras, Lent, Easter, Pentecost, a Summer Celebration of God's Creation, and Assumption.

Generations in Faith Together (GIFT). Faith Inkubators. This Sunday school system turns parents into the primary faith mentors, teachers, and faith role models for their own children, and surrounds families with extended, adopted faith families. Includes devotions for five nights at home.

Intergenerational Peacemaking Conferences. These annual conferences from the Presbyterian Peacemaking Program focus on peacemaking issues affecting our community, church, and world. To register or for more information, call Conference Registrar at 1-888-728-7228 x8700.

Molrine, Charlotte N., and Ronald C. Molrine. *Encountering Christ: An Intergenerational Faith Experience*. Morehouse Publishing, 1999. This 14-session programme includes group activities, role playing, and self-esteem exercises that aid in faith formation. This programme was written for confirmation or preparation for reception in the Episcopal Church.

O'Neal, Debbie Trafton. *The Family Hand-Me-Down Book: Ways to Build and Preserve History*. Augsburg Fortress, 2000. These ideas – spiritual histories, art throughout the generations, history quilt – explore ways to create stronger families by creating family histories.

Schut, Jessie. *I Believe: Getting Ready to Profess My Faith*. Faith Alive Christian Resources, 2004. Designed for students in grades five through eight, these eight sessions provide a guide to help mentors nurture the faith of young people.

Shouting in the Hush Arbor: An Afro-centric Intergenerational Program. Abingdon Press, 2005. This book contains church school lessons that encourage parents and children to learn about the Christian faith alongside one another.

Smith, Tim, Ed. *Family Sunday School Fun: 13 Bible Lessons for Children & Parents*. Group Publishing, 1999. These lessons include a Bible story time, snack and activity suggestions, and a covenant time. Although the title includes the word "fun," the lessons are highly discussion- and reading-based and the activities are suitable for older children only.

Stoner, Marcia Joslin. *Symbols of Faith: Teaching Images of the Christian Faith for Intergenerational Use.* Abingdon Press, 2001. This resource includes over 60 Christian symbols with activities for all ages designed to teach the background of each symbol. Reproducible patterns included for most symbols.

What Is This? Augsburg Fortress, 2001. These mentoring resources bring confirmation-age young people together with other persons of faith for candid conversation about faith and life.

Worshipping Together

Brown, Carolyn C. *You Can Preach to the Kids Too!: Designing Sermons for Adults and Children*. Abingdon Press, 1997. This book includes practical how-to advice such as presenting Scripture, shaping a sermon, and choosing illustrations that draw children in.

Children in the Sanctuary: Involving Children Fully in the Worship Life of a Congregation. Presbyterian Church, USA. This study guide and accompanying DVD include six segments on involving children fully in the worship life of your congregation.

Henderson, Dorothy. *Worship Together*. The Presbyterian Church in Canada, 1999. This ten-minute video shows how one congregation, as they did a monthly intergenerational worship service, includes an intergenerational team in planning, conducting, and evaluating the worship.

Macdonald, Ian, et al. *Worship for All Ages: Services for Special Sundays*. Wood Lake Books, 2005. When planning all-ages worship, this book provides creative and inspiring worship service outlines for Recovenanting Sunday, Worldwide Communion Sunday, Thanksgiving, All Saints' Day, Advent and Christmas (including Epiphany), Lent and Holy Week, and Easter and Pentecost.

Noel Series. Faith Alive Christian Resources. These reproducible intergenerational Christmas dramas in word and song include parts for children and adults. The series includes *Come to Bethlehem* (40 minutes); *Preparing the Way for Jesus* (50 minutes); *Good News from John* (60 minutes); *The Newborn King* (70 minutes); and *Return to the Stable* (75 minutes).

Wisdom, Andrew Carl. *Preaching to a Multi-Generational Assembly*. Liturgical Press, 2004. Designed especially for Roman Catholics, this book shows preachers how to use images and words to prepare sermons for many ages.

Serving Together

Lingo, Susan L. *101 Simple Service Projects Kids Can Do: Creative Ways to Touch Families, Communities, and the World!* Standard Publishing, 2000. In this book, children and adults will discover why God wants us to serve, and how serving others helps God. It contains mini fund raisers, simple service projects, and everyday acts of kindness.

Paratore, Coleen. *26 Big Things Small Hands*. Illustrated by Mike Reed. Free Spirit Publishing, 2004. A picture story book from A to Z exploring all the things small hands can do for others and the world.

Roehlkepartain, Jolene L. *Teaching Kids to Care & Share: 300+ Mission & Service Ideas for Children*. Abingdon Press, 2000. This book assumes that the spirit of service is born early in life, so the service suggestions start with age three. The book contains hundreds of inventive, hands-on ideas and activities for local churches, communities, and the world.

Web

Points of View. www.pointsofviewinc.com. James V. Gambone's site includes his much-admired Intergenerational Dialogue™ model.

Presbyterian Family and Intergenerational Ministries. www.pcusa.org/family.

Bible Story Books for Families or Christian Educators and Worship Leaders

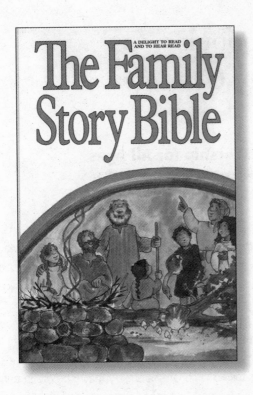

NEW

The Family Story Bible
Ralph Milton
Illustrated by Margaret Kyle

A Bible story book by gifted storyteller, Ralph Milton, that meets the expectations of today's values-oriented parents.

"A delight to read and to hear read. It is an open-ended story book, presenting endless possibilities for discussion with children. The beautiful illustrations are a far cry from the cartoonish pictures in so many children's Bible story books."

~ *The Presbyterian Record*

HC $19.95

Lectionary Story Bible (Year A)
Ralph Milton
Illustrated by Margaret Kyle

Once again, author Ralph Milton brings his enormous talent as a storyteller to the task of retelling biblical stories. Based on the best-selling *The Family Story Bible*, this first volume includes one or two stories for each Sunday of the year, based on the *Revised Common Lectionary* for Year A. An excellent resource for Christian educators, camp leaders, worship leaders, and families who want to share their faith at home.

$30.00
Year B, available 2008
Year C, available 2009

**Available from bookstores and resource centres
or call 1.800.663.2775 in Canada or visit www.woodlakebooks.com.
In the USA call 1.800.654.5129.**

From the popular
The Whole People of God Library!

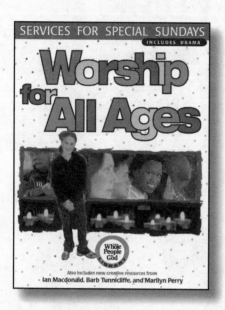

Worship for All Ages
Services for Special Sundays
Marilyn Perry

The key question in planning all ages worship is: "How can we share the bible passages and their message, visually and actively, in ways that will keep children involved as well as inspire adults?" *Worship for All Ages* is bursting with ideas to make your Intergenerational services come alive. Whether your congregation has a long history of all ages worship or is making a new commitment, *Worship for All Ages* will give you complete outlines and lots of ideas you can adapt to your unique situation. Includes resources from the best of *The Whole People of God* plus resources tested in congregations but never before in print. Organized around the Revised Common Lectionary, and identified for use in year A, B, or C.

$24.95 CAN | $19.95 USA

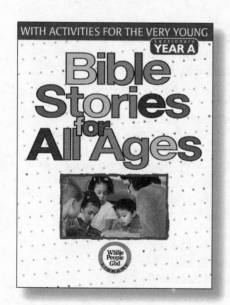

Bible Stories for All Ages
(Lectionary Year A)
With Activities for the Very Young

The first in this series– provides a year's worth of experiential bible stories for children aged 3 and up. Excellent for those responsible for bible stories in worship, for small churches with only a few children, and for intergenerational worship. Photocopiable activity sheets accompany each story to help children remember and retell the story in their own words.

$37.00 CAN | $34.00 USA

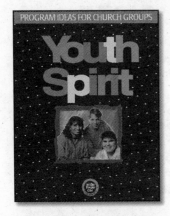

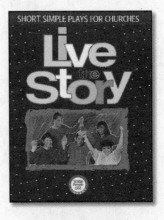

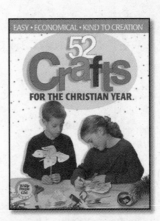

Books that Support your Ministry

A World of Faith
Introducing Spiritual Traditions to Teens
Carolyn Pogue

$29.95 CAN
$25.95 USA

A comprehensive book covering most of the world's main religions in a captivating and accessible way. Carolyn's emphasis goes beyond describing the unique practices of the various faith traditions, institutional rites and beliefs, to touch on the deeper truths common to humanity. Throughout there is a strong message of caring for the earth and for each other.

The Seasons of the Church Year Poster
Margaret Kyle, illustrator

$30.00

This useful teaching tool makes a great addition to any wall in your church or in your Sunday School classroom. The poster explains the flow of the church year by season, length, colour, and symbol. Beautiful, practical, and laminated for durability. Shipped in a tube.

Seasons Growing Faith
CD & Songbook Set
Donna Scorer &
Cathie Talbot, eds

Book and CD set
$28.95

Share the basics of the Christian faith with very young children. Enchanting, repetitive, easy-to-sing songs by Mary Lu Walker, Lesley Clare, Linnea Good, and other artists.

Seasons Growing Faith Board Book set
by Donna Scorer
Margaret Kyle, illustrator

Set of 5 $35.00

These sturdy board books are meant to be read over and over again to young children. The simple text and uncomplicated artwork will help young children experience and hear about a God of love and about the foundations of the Christian faith. Titles: God's Wonder World; Sing, David, Sing; Welcome Baby Jesus; Come Little Children; and Loving God Together. The books have rounded corners for safety.

The Bully & Me
Stories that Break the Cycle of Violence
Helen Carmichael Porter

$29.95 CAN | $24.95 USA

Helen Carmichael Porter has been telling her stories about victims and bullies for over eight years. The stories are based on Porter's observations, countless interviews, personal experience, and imagination and are helpful for children, parents, and educators. Includes a CD with 3 stories from the book told by the author – great for group listening and discussion.

Available from bookstores and resource centres
or call 1.800.663.2775 in Canada or visit www.woodlakebooks.com.
In the USA call 1.800.654.5129.